Behold the Man!

and Other Sermons

by
Oliver B. Greene

The Gospel Hour, Inc., Oliver B. Greene, Director
Box 2024, Greenville, South Carolina 29602

First printing, May 1970 — 15,000 copies
Second printing, December 1970 — 15,000 copies
Third printing, November 1973 — 15,000 copies
Fourth printing, September 1975 — 15,000 copies

$4.00

PREFACE

The sermons in this book relate to various subjects. Some of them were used in our tent meetings with success that brought glory to God.

It is our belief that the truths here presented are badly needed today, hence this book. May souls be won and Christians encouraged through the reading of these pages.

—The Author

PREFACE

Contents

Contents

Behold the Man!

Behold the Man!

"Then came Jesus forth, wearing the crown of thorns, and the purple robe. And Pilate saith unto them, *Behold the Man!*" (John 19:5).

Pilate's words are just as appropriate today as on the day they were spoken, the day Jesus was crucified. The singular need of this poor, sin-sick world is to *see Jesus*. He is the answer to every man's every need, the answer to the need of *every nation* under heaven. He alone can satisfy the hungry heart of mankind—restless, confused, perplexed, not knowing which way to turn or what to do. *The world today needs to behold JESUS.*

In the Old Testament we find the sacred admonition to Israel, *"Behold your GOD!"* (Isa. 40:9). In the very moment Israel took her eyes off Jehovah God, she began to commit idolatry. The people of Israel began to go after strange flesh. They began to intermarry with the enemies of God. They rebelled more and more, until finally God was forced to judge them and bring them back to Him through use of the chastening rod. The only way Israel could stay straight and walk in the paths of righteousness was to look steadfastly to God. *Beholding HIM* they walked in His statutes. When they turned their eyes from Him they went after the way of the flesh. There has been no change in man since then. Men still forget God and follow after the flesh—and yet, were it not for God we could not even exist!

God is the Author of all life. The universe in which we live testifies to the *fact* of God. The Psalmist testifies, "The *heavens* declare the glory of God, and the *firmament* sheweth His handywork. Day unto day uttereth speech, and night unto night sheweth knowledge. *There is no speech nor language where their voice is not heard*" (Psalm 19:1-3).

Psalm 24:1 declares, *"The EARTH is the Lord's, and the fulness thereof; the world, and they that dwell therein."*

A thinking person cannot walk in the sunlight of the day or in the silvery moonlight of the night without realizing that there is a God behind this heavenly splendor. Some unregenerate minds would have us believe that this earth just "happened," that creation simply "evolved," or that by some freakish and accidental rearrangement of matter the earth and planets merely "came into existence." By such philosophy, we who believe in *God* are immediately branded as fools!

But no! This earth, the stars, the moon, the sun—this entire glorious universe—did not just "happen." They are the products of the creative hand of our God (Gen. 1:1; Heb. 1:1, 2). Men of wisdom look at the stars and know there is a God behind them. It is the *fool* who "hath said in his heart, There is no God!" (Psalm 53:1). According to God's Word, the man who declares *"There is no God"* is announcing to the world that he is a fool. It might be in order to commend him, for at least he is announcing his spiritual and mental ignorance and his utter foolishness! This frankness does not characterize some of the men in pulpits today, because *they* do not *announce their identity.* They prefer to work on both sides of the fence— but God demands undivided and complete loyalty and condones no divided allegiance. Jesus declared, "He that is not *with* me is *against* me; and he that gathereth not with me scattereth abroad" (Matt. 12:30).

There is a lack of God-consciousness even among professed Christians today. When we examine present-day Christianity we usually find a great deal of religious zeal and fervor, but the emphasis and direction are wrong. Many "religious" people are being distracted from the chief objective of their religion—an objective which, in Christianity, must be nothing short of God Himself. The fundamental fact of Christianity is that "Christ also hath once suffered for sins, the just for the unjust, *that He might bring us to God . . .*" (I Pet. 3:18). The born again believer is dead unto sin but "alive unto GOD through Jesus Christ our Lord" (Rom. 6:11). But in most churches today the emphasis

11

is on "program," organization, education, tradition, baptism, man-made dogma and teachings of men.

You see, the devil does not care how long nor how loud a man preaches—nor how many "good works" he carries on—as long as he detours around the Christ, the love of God, and the power of the blood! Many Christians today are so busy, so occupied, with *the things of GOD,* that they are *forgetting the GOD OF THINGS.* The majority of "religious" folk today are too busy with church activities to pay any attention to God. Plans are made a year in advance, the program is set up, committees are appointed, membership drives are planned—and as a matter of fact, in many churches there is not much *need* for God! Committees and paid workers handle the program, while the congregation is busy keeping the "machinery" oiled and running.

Instead of being called of God, many preachers today are being turned out of denominational seminaries in much the same way an automobile manufacturer turns cars off the assembly line—i. e., the cars differ in body style, and that is about all the difference there is in *denominationally-trained preachers.* They differ in "body styles," but head and heart are the same. They are in the denominational "groove," they preach what they are trained to preach, they build their sermons to suit the denominational bosses, and they are told that in order to be successful they must "go along with the program."

The Apostle Paul was a good example of a very successful preacher. He determined not to *know or preach* anything but *"CHRIST, and Him crucified!"* (I Cor. 2:2). Oh, yes—I know Paul paid for his preaching with his life. His faithfulness to Christ cost him his head! He won a martyr's crown, *"a crown of righteousness"* (II Tim. 4:8); and if he had had a *thousand* lives to give, it is my conviction that he would gladly have given them *all* for the privilege of preaching the Christ who shed His blood for the remission of sin!

Another grave danger to which we are exposed in these closing days of grace is the danger of beholding *"experiences,"* while failing to behold the God who is the Giver of all *true spiritual experiences.* Much emphasis is being put on "emotion" today. Do not misunderstand me—no one believes in a heartfelt salvation more strongly than I do; but we are not saved by "feelings," and emotions do not guarantee the genuineness of a spiritual experience. The *devil* can produce "feelings"—yes, even "good" feelings; but he cannot produce saving faith. Salvation does not come by a "thrill," a chill up the spine. *The grace of GOD brings salvation* (Tit. 2:11). Some people declare that they are saved simply because they have had an answer to prayer, or because they had a "vision" or saw a light—but hear this, beloved:

God's Word warns, "Believe not every spirit, but try the spirits whether they are of God: because many false prophets are gone out into the world" (I John 4:1).

Salvation is not "Behold your *creed,*" or "Behold your *theology,*" or "Behold your *denomination,*" or "Behold your *experience.*" Salvation is from *without*—salvation is *of God.* Therefore, *"Behold your God"*—or, as Pilate said to the Jews on that fateful day, *"BEHOLD THE MAN"—the Man CHRIST JESUS!*

Behold Him as a PERSON:—

Thank God, Jesus is a Person. He is not an "influence" or a spirit. As the second Person in the Godhead, He was with God in the beginning (John 1:1, 2, 14). He was in the bosom of the Father (John 1:18). But God's Christ who became man's Jesus took a body of flesh, a body of humiliation like unto the body of sinful man, and came into this world to do a work for us. He took a body (Heb. 10:5) and in that body He paid the sin-debt, that we might have life and have it abundantly. The Gospel of John, the "salvation Gospel," was written that we might believe that Jesus is the Christ, the Son of God; and believing, we might have life through His name (John 20:31).

The very proof of Christianity is *the Man Christ Jesus.* Christianity has proof that Christ came back from the dead. In Revelation 1:18 the glorified

Christ Himself declares, *"I am He that liveth, and was dead; and, behold, I am ALIVE for evermore,* Amen; and have the keys of hell and of death!"* No other religion on earth can make such a claim.

There have been many great religious leaders, there have been numerous founders of religions— but Jesus was neither. He did not come into the world to become a religious leader, nor to found a new religion. He came to bring salvation down to man and to purchase salvation for all who will come unto God by Him. He came into this world as a Person, He lived and died as a Person, and as the Man Christ Jesus He now sits at the right hand of God as our Mediator, *the ONE Mediator between God and man* (I Tim. 2:5).

Behold Him POSITIONALLY:—

The Man Christ Jesus is now exalted to the highest seat in heaven. When He had "by Himself purged our sins," He sat down *"on the right hand of the Majesty on high"* (Heb. 1:3).

Peter said to the Jews, "Let all the house of Israel know *assuredly,* that God hath made *that SAME JESUS,* whom ye have crucified, *BOTH LORD AND CHRIST"* (Acts 2:36).

The *despised* Man is now *the exalted Man.* He "made Himself of no reputation, and took upon Him the form of a servant, and was made in the likeness of men: and being found in fashion as a man, He humbled Himself, and became obedient

15

unto death, even the death of the cross. *WHERE-FORE God also hath highly EXALTED Him,* and given Him a name which is above every name: that at the name of Jesus every knee should bow, of things in heaven, and things in earth, and things under the earth; and that every tongue should confess that Jesus Christ is Lord, to the glory of God the Father" (Phil. 2:7-11). Truly, "the Stone which the builders *disallowed,* the same is made *the head of the corner"* (I Pet. 2:7).

Behold Him MYSTICALLY:—

"The Christ" in a mystical sense signifies Christ and the members of His body—that is, every born again person is a member of the body of Christ (Eph. 5:30). Christ is the head of the Church (Eph. 5:23). He is the foundation of the Church (I Cor. 3:11), and all believers are baptized into His body by the Holy Spirit (I Cor. 12:12, 13). Christ is the *fulness* of the Church (Col. 2:9, 10), and the Church is the fulness of Christ (Eph. 1:23). Christ and the Church cannot be separated. The Church is the body, and Christ is the *head,* the *foundation,* and the *life* of the New Testament Church, of which all believers are members.

Behold Him REPRESENTATIVELY:—

Believers are identified with Christ: "There is therefore now no condemnation to them which are *in Christ Jesus . . ."* (Rom. 8:1). Christ is identified with believers—"*Christ in you,* the hope of glory" (Col. 1:27). We are crucified with Christ, we died with Him (Gal. 2:20); but we are also risen with Christ and alive unto God (Rom. 6:1-11). We have been quickened together with Christ, and in Him we "sit together in heavenly places" (Eph. 2:5, 6).

Behold Him PROVISIONALLY:—

In Christ the believer finds an abundance of "all spiritual blessings" (Eph. 1:3). *Apart* from Christ, we cannot expect God to bless us. Jesus promised, "Seek ye first the kingdom of God, and *HIS righteousness;* and *all these things will be ADDED unto you*" (Matt. 6:33). Jesus was God manifest in the flesh (II Cor. 5:19), and Jesus is the *righteousness* of God (I Cor. 1:30). *IN Christ, ALL THINGS are ours* (I Cor. 3:22, 23), but if we refuse to put first things first, we cannot expect God to keep His promise to us.

Behold Him POTENTIALLY:—

Not "creed" but CHRIST is the secret of the Christian life. Not dogma, not doctrine—but *Christ WITHIN* is the only way in which Christ-like living can be accomplished. Baptism, sincerity, doing our best—none of these will give us victory in the Christian walk. We *live* differently because Christ dwells within our hearts in the Person of the Holy Spirit. Victory in the Christian life comes not by Christ AND the believer, but by *Christ IN the*

17

believer—"greater is He (Christ) that is in you, than he (the devil) that is in the world" (I John 4:4).

"As many as are led by the Spirit of God, they are the sons of God" (Rom. 8:14). We are *"MORE than conquerors* through Him that loved us" (Rom. 8:37). Christ and Christ alone gives victory. It makes no difference how many pledges we may sign, how many promises we may make, nor how hard we may try to be all that we ought to be; if Christ is not *in the heart,* no man can live a Christ-like life!

Behold Him PROPHETICALLY:—

"For the Lord Himself shall descend from heaven with a shout, with the voice of the archangel, and with the trump of God: *and THE DEAD IN CHRIST shall rise first"* (I Thess. 4:16).

Christ is our guarantee of resurrection. "For as in Adam all die, even so in Christ shall all be made alive—but every man in his own order: *Christ the FIRSTFRUITS;* afterward they that are Christ's at His coming" (I Cor. 15:22, 23). The fact of Christ's resurrection guarantees that we will rise bodily from the grave.

The moment a believer dies, his body returns to the dust and his spirit returns "unto God who gave it" (Eccl. 12:7). To be absent from the body is to be present with the Lord (II Cor. 5:6, 8; Phil. 1:23). But when Jesus comes for His Church, believers will be raised incorruptible (I Cor. 15:52), and we will be given a body like unto the glorious resurrection body of Jesus (I John 3:2).

God cannot die. Therefore God became man (II Cor. 5:19), when Christ took a body of humiliation like unto the body of sinful man in order that He might die for our sin, "that He by the grace of God should taste death for every man" (Heb. 2:9). The Man Christ Jesus now sits at the right hand of God the Father (Heb. 1:3) and intercedes for us. He is our Mediator—the *only* Mediator between God and man (I Tim. 2:5). *And "this SAME JESUS"* will come again (Acts 1:11) to redeem our bodies and fashion them "like unto His glorious body, according to the working whereby He is able even to subdue all things unto Himself" (Phil. 3:21). Yes, Christ is our guarantee of the resurrection of the dead—"for the hour is coming, in the which all that are in the graves shall hear His voice, and shall come forth; they that have done good, unto the resurrection of life (which is the resurrection of the saints, the *first* resurrection, the wicked dead to be raised one thousand years later); and they that have done evil, unto the resurrection of damnation" (John 5:28, 29).

"Behold the MAN"—but let us also behold a few of the statements made about this Man:

1. *"Never man spake like THIS Man"* (John 7:46).

These words would not seem so strange if they

had been spoken by the mother of Jesus, or by John the Baptist, or by one of the disciples of Jesus. But they were spoken by the officers who had been sent to arrest Him. The Pharisees decided that it was about time to stop the mouth of this street preacher from Nazareth. They said among themselves, "Behold, the world is gone after Him!" (John 12:19). So they sent officers to arrest Jesus, and when they returned without Him, the chief priests and Pharisees asked, "Why have ye not brought Him?" The officers replied, "Never man spake like THIS Man!" (Please read John 7:40-53).

I am convinced that when the officers arrived where Jesus was preaching, they stopped long enough to listen to His wonderful words of life. They heard Him invite, "If any man thirst, let him come unto me, and drink. He that believeth on me, as the Scripture hath said, out of his belly shall flow rivers of living water!" He was speaking of the Holy Spirit, who had not yet come into the world (John 7:37-39).

If the officers had arrested Jesus the moment they walked up to where He was preaching, they might have been able to take Him; but they listened to His words, His words arrested their hearts, and they could not arrest Him. They returned to the Pharisees and explained, "We could not arrest a man who talked as this Man does. His words are different. We have never before heard words like He spoke."

How true! Jesus Himself declared, *"The words that I speak unto you, they are spirit, and they are LIFE"* (John 6:63). There have been great teachers, great preachers, great religious leaders— but who among them would dare to announce, "If any man thirst, let him come unto me, and drink"? Who but the Lord Jesus Christ would dare invite, "Come unto me, all ye that labour and are heavy laden, and I will give you rest"? Or "Him that cometh to me, I will in no wise cast out"? or "My sheep know my voice . . . I give unto them eternal life, and they shall never perish"? And even if any man dared make such a sta.ement he could not live up to his promise!

But Jesus has never broken a promise. He is God—and God cannot lie (Tit. 1:2; Heb. 6:18), and any person who will read the New Testament account of the life, ministry, and miracles of Jesus —the things He did and the words He spoke—will be convinced that He was no ordinary man. He is the Christ of God, extraordinary in all that He did and said. *This Man*, the Man Christ Jesus, is *ample proof* that Christianity is real! Never man spake like this Man!

2. *"This Man receiveth sinners..."* (Luke 15:2).

This remark was made by those who would be least expected to criticize Jesus for receiving sinners. It was not the reprobate, unlearned, despicable characters of that day who made the statement here. It was the religious leaders, the scribes and Pharisees. They themselves *should* have been interested in sinners. They considered that they were the sole custodians of the oracles of God, and they should have been concerned about those who did not know God. But instead, they murmured against Jesus because He received sinners into His presence, and *ate* with them—something an orthodox Jew would never have done!

But are we so very different today? Most Christians are not interested in the welfare of the lost. They have their own small circle of Christian friends who occupy their time, and the scope of their interest *ends* there. They have a wonderful time of fellowship—but what of the *unsaved* around us? Should we never *include them* in our thoughts and plans? Should we never tell them about the Bread of Life and point them to the Lamb of God who saves sinners? We could win souls to Christ if we only put forth the effort and showed some interest in them.

Do not misunderstand me. I am not recommending that Christians renew fellowship with the world—no indeed! But Jesus visited the homes of both saved and unsaved, and He never entered any home except in the interest of the spiritual welfare of those who lived there! Even in the home of Mary, Martha, and Lazarus He taught of "that good part" which Mary had chosen and which would not be taken away from her (Luke

10:42).

He called Zacchaeus down from the sycamore tree, telling him, "Make haste, and come down; for to day I must abide at thy house" (Luke 19:5). He was criticized for being "guest with a man that is a sinner," but the overall result of that fellowship was that Zacchaeus was saved, and proved his change of heart by his testimony: "Lord, the half of my goods I give to the poor; and if I have taken anything from any man by false accusation, I restore him fourfold." Jesus then said to him, "This day is salvation come to this house!" (Read Luke 19:1-10.)

There is entirely too much selfishness among God's people today. Believers enjoy the fellowship of other believers—and that is as it should be. There is nothing wrong with rejoicing in the Lord. But Jesus said, *"Herein is my Father glorified, that ye bear much fruit; so shall ye be my disciples"* (John 15:8). We glorify God when we win souls— but if we hope to win sinners to Christ we must go where they are. We cannot sit and wait for the unsaved to come to us. We are instructed to go out "into the highways and hedges, and compel them to come in" (Luke 14:23).

It is true that Christians are not *OF the world* and we are not to be conformed *to* the world; but if we lead souls to Christ we will certainly have to go in search of them—that is, we will not find them in Christian fellowship nor in fine, fashionable churches. We must go for them, go with a determination to win them. We must go in the name of Him who said, *"Go ye* into all the world, and preach the Gospel to every creature" (Mark 16:15). Christ died for sinners, and it is to His glory that He has given us the glorious opportunity of rescuing men from hell and pointing them toward heaven.

3. *"I find no fault in THIS MAN"* (Luke 23:4).

We might think, "Surely these words were spoken by someone who loved Jesus very much—His mother, John the Beloved, someone from the home of Mary, Martha, and Lazarus"—but not so. They were spoken by a man who had a wicked heart— Pilate the Roman governor. Not once but *three times* during the trial of Jesus, Pilate made the statement, "I find *no fault* in Him!" (John 18:38; 19:4, 6).

Has there ever been another "faultless" one? Has there ever been another person who could challenge his enemies, "Which of you convinceth me of sin?" (John 8:46). Not one of the enemies of Jesus could bring against Him any proof of wrong-doing; and when He was brought to trial they were forced to hire false witnesses to testify against Him!

Not only is Jesus sinless, holy, and righteous; but *in HIM* the *believer* finds holiness. We are instructed, "Follow peace with all men, *and HO-LINESS*, without which no man shall see the

Lord" (Heb. 12:14). But where can we *obtain* holiness? Do we gain it by good living, or by good works or good behavior? No indeed! God's Word answers: *"Of Him are ye IN Christ Jesus, who of God is made unto us wisdom, and RIGHTEOUSNESS, and sanctification, and redemption"* (I Cor. 1:30).

We have holiness because we have Christ, and His holiness has been imparted to us. Our own righteousnesses are as filthy rags (Isa. 64:6). Without holiness no man shall see God, but our holiness is in THIS MAN whom Pilate declared to be faultless, and against whom not even His worst enemies could prove an accusation of sin.

Dear reader, do *you* know Jesus as your Saviour? Have you beheld Him as He died on a cross for your sin? Have you beheld Him as He stretches forth His nail-pierced hand, inviting "whosoever will" to come to Him and be saved? If you do not know Him in forgiveness of your sins, I beg you to accept Him into your heart, that His holiness may be imputed to you; and when you stand before God you will be found *"complete in HIM"* (Col. 2:10).

4. *"Truly THIS MAN was the Son of God"* (Mark 15:39).

For six long hours the Roman centurion had been gazing upon the Man on the middle cross. We find Mark's account of the crucifixion in Mark's Gospel, chapter 15, verses 24-39. The soldiers gambled for the Lord's garments. The superscription over His head read, "THE KING OF THE JEWS." Two thieves were crucified with Him— one on the right, the other on the left. The passing crowds mocked the Man on the middle cross. The chief priests and the scribes mocked Him— "He saved others; Himself He cannot save!"

Darkness settled over the land—and "at the ninth hour Jesus cried with a loud voice, saying... My God, my God! Why hast thou forsaken me? ... And one ran and filled a spunge full of vinegar, and put it on a reed, and gave Him to drink. . . . And Jesus cried with a loud voice, and gave up the ghost. And the veil of the temple was rent in twain from the top to the bottom. *And when the centurion, which stood over against Him, saw that He so cried out, and gave up the ghost, he said, TRULY THIS MAN WAS THE SON OF GOD!*"

What convinced the centurion that Jesus was the Son of God? "Faith cometh by hearing, and hearing by the Word of God" (Rom. 10:17). Jesus was God in flesh. Therefore *whatever* His words, they were the words of God. During the time Jesus hung on the cross, He spoke seven times— and the centurion standing nearby heard His words. Then you will notice the Scripture tells us that Jesus "cried with *a loud voice.*" Dying men do not cry with a loud voice, nor do ordinary men die at will, as when Jesus passed His spirit back into the hands of His heavenly Father. So the centurion not only heard the *words* of Jesus, he also heard the cry of victory and witnessed the supernatural things that took place when the Man on the middle cross declared, *"It is finished!"* and bowed His head and gave up the ghost (John 19:30).

Hearing the words of Jesus and witnessing His death, the centurion was convinced that he had witnessed the death of the Son of God—and he gave his testimony to that fact. The Scriptures declare, "No man can say that Jesus is the Lord, but by the Holy Ghost" (I Cor. 12:3). I John 4:15 says, "Whosoever shall confess that Jesus is the Son of God, God dwelleth in him, and he in God." The centurion testified, *"Truly this Man was the Son of God,"* and I personally believe he went away from the cross a saved man.

Unsaved friend, *behold the Man*—this Man who of His own free will died on the cross for the sin of the whole world, that whosoever would believe on Him and accept His finished work might be saved! Behold the Christ of God—and *live*. Refuse to behold Him as the Christ of God—and be *forever damned*. "He that believeth on Him is not condemned: but *he that believeth NOT is condemned ALREADY*, because he hath not believed in the name of the only begotten Son of God" (John 3:18).

5. *". . . God hath made that same Jesus . . .*

both Lord and Christ" (Acts 2:36).

These words are part of one of the greatest sermons ever preached. Peter was the spokesman, fresh from Pentecost. As a result of this sermon (recorded in Acts 2:14-41) three thousand souls were saved and added to the Church.

Peter reminded the Jews of how David had prophesied concerning the coming of God's Christ, and how David declared that God would raise Jesus from the dead (Psalm 16:10). The heart of Peter's message was, "This Man—this same Jesus —whom you fellows nailed to the cross, has risen from the dead *and God has made Him BOTH LORD AND CHRIST."*

The death, burial, and resurrection of Jesus "according to the Scriptures" is the Gospel which leads sinners to become sons of God (I Cor. 15:1-4). It was the death, burial, and resurrection of Jesus that Peter preached to the Jews that day, driving home the truth that opened their eyes, broke their hearts, and caused them to cry out, *"Men and brethren, what shall we DO?"* (Acts 2:37).

The death, burial, and resurrection of Jesus "according to the Scriptures" is the Gospel that brings men to Christ. "If thou shalt confess with thy mouth the Lord Jesus, and shalt *believe in thine heart that God hath raised Him from the dead, THOU SHALT BE SAVED"* (Rom. 10:9). This is the verse that changed me from a sinner into a child of God and a preacher of the Gospel.

It is the same truth which Peter preached on the Day of Pentecost when three thousand souls were saved.

There have been many great religious leaders. Many names in the field of religion have left their mark upon the civilization of the entire world—leaders like Mohammed, Confucius, Mary Baker Eddy, Rutherford, and others; but no other religious group on earth claims that their leader rose from the dead! Only Christianity makes that claim. Furthermore, the Word of God declares, "If Christ be not risen, then is our preaching vain, and your faith is also vain.... And if Christ be not raised . . . ye are yet in your sins. Then they also which are fallen asleep in Christ are perished! . . . *But now IS Christ risen from the dead, and become the firstfruits of them that slept*" (I Cor. 15:14-20 in part).

6. "*. . . through THIS MAN is preached unto you the forgiveness of sins*" (Acts 13:38).

These words were spoken by a man who at one time despised the very name of Jesus, a man who persecuted the Church, consigned Christians to prison, and consented to the stoning of Stephen. Yes, the Apostle Paul delivered the words just quoted, when he preached to the Jews at Antioch in Pisidia.

In verse 39 of that same passage we read, "And *BY HIM all that believe are justified from all things*, from which ye could not be justified by the law of Moses." These men to whom Paul was speaking were sticklers for the law of Moses; but Paul did not hesitate to tell them that this Man Jesus (whom they had crucified) was able to do for them what the law of Moses never had done and never could do—that is, *by HIM, ALL who believe are justified from ALL things*. This statement concerning justification through the righteousness of Christ was hard for the Jews to accept—and even for mankind today it is still regarded with misgiving and distrust.

Do you know what it means to be *justified*? It has been said that to be justified is to be "just as though you had never sinned." In other words, to be justified in God's sight is to be just as just as *Jesus* is just. It is His blood which brings justification and cleanses from all sin (I John 1:7). To be cleansed from all sin is to be holy, sinless, and pure in God's sight—but such standing comes only through THIS MAN, this same Jesus who died on the cross. "Therefore we conclude that a man is justified by faith without the deeds of the law" (Rom. 3:28). Jesus was "delivered for our offences, and was raised again for our justification. Therefore being justified by faith, we have peace with God through our Lord Jesus Christ" (Rom. 4:25; 5:1).

Through "this Man" (Jesus) is preached the forgiveness of sins. All others are thieves and robbers. He is the Way, the Truth, and the Life.

No man can come to God except through Him. "Neither is there salvation in any other: for there is none other name under heaven given among men, whereby we MUST be saved" (Acts 4:12).

7. *"THIS MAN . . . offered one sacrifice for sins for ever . . ."* (Heb. 10:12).

Under the Mosaic law, the high priest offered sacrifices again and again for the sins of the people—as well as for his own sins. But the blood of bulls and goats could never take away sins (Heb. 10:4). Every drop of blood offered on altars in the Old Testament pointed to the blood of the Lamb of God who would one day shed His blood on the cross of Calvary. If God had not given Jesus a body (Heb. 10:5) in which He could die, the sin-debt would never have been paid, all the blood offered by the high priests under the law would have been offered in vain, and we of today would be in our sins and on the road to hell!

But—*glorious truth*—"by one offering He (this Man, Jesus) hath perfected for ever them that are sanctified. Whereof the Holy Ghost also is a witness to us: for after that He had said before, This is the covenant that I will make with them after those days, saith the Lord: I will put my laws into their hearts, and in their minds will I write them; and their *sins and iniquities* will I remember no more. *Now where remission of these is, there is NO MORE OFFERING FOR SIN"* (Heb. 10: 14-18).

Thank God, because of the all-sufficient and once-for-all sacrifice Christ made for us, we do not need to return year after year to offer another sacrifice. We do not need to come again and again to beg redemption from sin. Christ purged our sin *once*, forever. (I am speaking of *SIN—singular*—the sin of unbelief which damns the soul, the sin John the Baptist pointed out when he said of Jesus, "Behold the Lamb of God, which taketh away *the SIN of the world*"—John 1:29.)

We are invited to confess our *"sins"* (plural), which include the sins of omission as well as those of commission; and when we confess our sins "He is faithful and just to forgive us our sins, and to cleanse us from all unrighteousness" (I John 1:9).

The sin-debt has been paid, redemption has been purchased; but as long as we remain in these tabernacles of flesh we will be subject to faults and failures; and nothing less than perfect, spotless holiness will satisfy God. Such perfection and holiness are found only in the finished work of the Lord Jesus Christ, and nothing short of His finished work and His shed blood will make us fit for the kingdom of God.

Sinner friend, you have not one thing to offer God but your sinful self; but if you will offer yourself to God in the name of Jesus, He will receive you *for Christ's sake.* You could never offer God enough good works, good living, money or time to satisfy His righteous demands. He is satisfied

only in Christ, and what He does for you and for
me is all made possible because the Man Christ
Jesus took our place and paid our sin-debt.

God has not changed His mind about sin. He
still thunders out, *"The soul that sinneth, it shall
DIE!"* (Ezek. 18:4). God has no more respect for
sin today than He had the day He drove Adam
and Eve from the Garden of Eden (Gen. 3:24), or
when He sent the judgment of the flood upon sinful man to destroy him from the face of the earth.
Only Noah and his family were saved—Noah who
"found grace in the eyes of the Lord" (Gen. 6:8)—
and that same grace brought Jesus down to man
for the express purpose of dying for the sin of the
world. Therefore, *God's grace imparted to you* is
the only way in which you can prevent His judgment from falling upon you.

"We see JESUS, who was made a little lower
than the angels for the suffering of death, crowned
with glory and honour; *that He by THE GRACE
OF GOD should taste death for EVERY MAN"*
(Heb. 2:9). The wages of sin is *death* (Rom. 6:23),
and the soul that sinneth shall surely die! But by
the grace of God, Jesus tasted death for every man,
for ALL men—and *"this Man,* after He had offered
one sacrifice for sins FOR EVER, sat down on
the right hand of God; from henceforth expecting
till His enemies be made His footstool. For *by
ONE offering* He hath *perfected FOR EVER* them
that are sanctified" (Heb. 10:12-14).

33

Rituals, religious activity, offerings, good works, faithful church attendance—none of these will save us. Certainly these are good things and we should observe them—not in order to *be saved*, but because we *are* saved. I do not preach the Gospel and try to win souls in order to go to heaven. I preach the Gospel and labor day by day to win souls because of the fact that I myself am saved; and having found salvation myself, I want to see others saved.

Going to heaven is as simple as receiving Jesus: "As many as *received Him,* to them gave He power to become the sons of God, even to them that believe on His name" (John 1:12).

Going to *hell* is as simple as *rejecting* Jesus: ". . . he that *believeth not* is *condemned already,* because he hath not believed in the name of the only begotten Son of God" (John 3:18).

God loved sinners so much that He gave His only begotten Son to die for the sin of the world (John 3:16).

Jesus loved sinners so much that He willingly left the bosom of the Father and the glories of heaven, to come to earth and lay down His life that we might be saved through faith in His sacrifice (John 10:17, 18).

All who are so ungrateful for God's love and mercy as to live their lives without Him, refusing to confess Jesus as Saviour, will be forced to confess Him at the judgment on that great and terrible day of the Lord. Yes, God has "appointed a day, *in the which He will judge the world in righteousness by THAT MAN* whom He hath ordained; whereof He hath given assurance unto all men, in that He hath raised Him from the dead" (Acts 17:31).

God's Word further declares, "It is written, *As I live,* saith the Lord, *EVERY KNEE shall bow to me, and EVERY TONGUE shall confess to God"* (Rom. 14:11). As sure as God lives, every soul will meet Him—either "accepted in the Beloved" (Eph. 1:6), or *without* the salvation purchased by the precious blood of Jesus. *Which will it be for YOU, dear reader?*

Behold the Man who declared, "He that rejecteth me, and receiveth not my words, hath One that judgeth him: *the WORD that I have spoken, the same shall judge him in the last day"* (John 12:48). And what are some of the words of Jesus by which we will be judged? We cannot of course quote all of the passages, but we will look at just a few:

Luke 13:3 and 5: "Except ye repent, ye shall all likewise perish."

John 5:39, 40: "Search the Scriptures; for in them ye think ye have eternal life: and they are they which testify of me. And ye will not come to me, that ye might have life."

Matthew 5:20: "Except your righteousness shall exceed the righteousness of the scribes and Pharisees, ye shall in no case enter into the kingdom of heaven."

Matthew 18:3: "Verily I say unto you, Except ye be converted, and become as little children, ye shall not enter into the kingdom of heaven."

Mark 9:43-48: "If thy hand offend thee, cut it off: it is better for thee to enter into life maimed, than having two hands to go into hell, into the fire that never shall be quenched: where their worm dieth not, and the fire is not quenched. And if thy foot offend thee, cut it off: it is better for thee to enter halt into life, than having two feet to be cast into hell, into the fire that never shall be quenched: where their worm dieth not, and the fire is not quenched. And if thine eye offend thee, pluck it out: it is better for thee to enter into the kingdom of God with one eye, than having two eyes to be cast into hell fire, where their worm dieth not, and the fire is not quenched!"

These last words were taken from what I consider to be the strongest, most direct sermon ever preached on the fires of hell, the message delivered by none other than the Lord Jesus Christ and recorded in Mark chapter 9. Jesus believed in an everlasting hell—and regardless of what the *"worm"* may be, He makes it very plain that it is the part of man that will never die. For the unsaved, this means everlasting torment in the fires of hell! But the words of Jesus also invite, *"Come unto me, all ye that labour and are heavy laden, and I will*

give you rest. Take my yoke upon you, and learn
of me; for I am meek and lowly in heart: and ye
shall find rest unto your souls. For my yoke is
easy, and my burden is light" (Matt. 11:28-30).

John 7:37,38: "If any man thirst, let him come
unto me and drink. He that believeth on me, as
the Scripture hath said, out of his belly shall flow
rivers of living water."

John 6:51: "I am the living bread which came
down from heaven. If any man eat of this bread,
he shall live for ever . . . ."

John 6:35,37: "I am the bread of life. He that
cometh to me shall never hunger; and he that believeth on me shall never thirst. . . . and him that
cometh to me I will in no wise cast out."

The words of Jesus will judge you, dear reader,
if you do not accept the Christ who uttered them.
I urge you to *behold the Man* who spoke a message unlike any other message ever spoken—"Come
unto me, and *I will give you rest!*" No other
person could make that statement to poor, troubled
humanity—and expect to make it come true. Only
Jesus could do that. His message is singular in
every respect. His invitation stands alone.

Behold the Man who did what no other man
would dare to do—He declared His equality with
Almighty God: "He that hath seen me hath seen
the Father" (John 14:9).

Behold the Man who defied all laws of medi-
cine, science, and the elements. He touched and

cleansed the lepers (Matt. 8:2-4; Luke 17:12-19). He raised the dead (John 11:38-44; Luke 7:11-15; Matt. 9:18-26). He spoke peace to the wind and the waves and they obeyed Him (Luke 8:22-25). He walked across the water to join His disciples in a ship in the midst of a storm-tossed sea (Matt. 14:24-27).

Behold the Man who offers to men what no mortal has ever dared offer, or ever could offer—forgiveness of sins. Salvation is a finished, historical fact. Jesus paid the sin-debt. He took all the sins of all the world and nailed them to His cross. He settled the sin question *once, for all, FOREVER.* He alone can forgive sins, and He also furnishes the evidence that guilt is gone! He removes sins and gives peace (John 14:27).

Behold this Man who was in the beginning with God (John 1:1, 2), who willingly took upon Himself the form of a servant, came into the world and laid down His life for sinners (Rom. 5:8; Phil. 2:6-8).

Behold this Man who tasted death for all men (Heb. 2:9), descended into the Paradise compartment of hell (Matt. 12:38-42; Acts 2:27; Eph. 4:8-10), and took from the devil the keys of death and hell (Heb. 2:14; Rev. 1:18). He walked out of the tomb and appeared unto men for forty days after His resurrection (Acts 1:3).

Behold this Man who, as His disciples gazed upon Him, was taken up into heaven (Acts 1:9) and even now is seated at the right hand of God as the only Mediator between God and man (Heb. 1:3; I Tim. 2:5).

Behold this Man who even today invites "whosoever will" to come to Him for life, rest, peace, and an eternal home with Him in heaven. But dear sinner friend, if you *refuse* to come to Him for life, then you must suffer eternal death in the lake of fire that burns with brimstone. God's Word declares that the "fearful, *and UNBELIEVING,* and the abominable, and murderers, and whoremongers, and sorcerers, and idolaters, and all liars, shall have their part in the lake which burneth with fire and brimstone: which is the second death" (Rev. 21:8).

Behold the Man whom to know aright is life eternal. He looks your way with tender love, longing to save you. He is able to save you, and He will save you this very moment if you will bow your head, confess your sins, and ask Him to forgive and save you. "Believe on the Lord Jesus Christ, and thou shalt be saved!" (Acts 16:31).

**The Saddest, the Most Important,
the Most Glorious Passages In the Bible**

The Saddest, the Most Important, the Most Glorious Passages In the Bible

You may not agree that the three passages I have chosen are the saddest, the most important, and the most glorious passages in all the Word of God, but you will surely agree with what I say about them because I am going to give line upon line, truth upon truth, as it is laid down in God's holy Word. We may not agree on the subject, but we will agree on the truth presented.

I
The Saddest Passage In the Bible

"Not every one that saith unto me, Lord, Lord, shall enter into the kingdom of heaven; but he that doeth the will of my Father which is in heaven. Many will say to me in that day, Lord, Lord, have we not prophesied in thy name? and in thy name have cast out devils? and in thy name done many wonderful works? And then will I profess unto them, I never knew you: depart from me, ye that work iniquity" (Matt. 7:21-23).

To me, in all the Bible we find no sadder words than those in the verses just quoted. There are three things here that I want us to see clearly:

1. Not everyone who cries "Lord, Lord!" shall enter the kingdom of heaven.

Believing with "head belief" and crying unto the Lord does not save us nor make us ready for the kingdom of heaven. "The *devils* believe, and tremble" (James 2:19), but we know they are not saved. We are not saved by what we *say*, but by what we *do*. We are saved because of a living faith born in the heart by hearing the precious Word of God. *"Faith* cometh by *hearing,* and hearing by the Word of God" (Rom. 10:17). So— not all will be saved who cry "Lord, Lord," but those who do *the will of God;* and if we do not do God's will we will not be saved no matter how long or how loud we pray, no matter how many "good works" we may do.

And what IS the WILL OF GOD? Jesus Himself answers that question. In John 6:40 He declared, *"THIS is the will of Him that sent me,* that every one which *seeth the Son, and believeth on Him,* may have everlasting life: and I will raise him up at the last day." This verse plainly tells me that the will of God the Father concerning me is that I believe on His Son, the Lord Jesus Christ, whom God sent into the world to pay the sin debt and purchase my redemption.

The only possible way for a person to be saved is through Jesus. "Neither is there salvation in any other: for there is *none other name* under heaven given among men, *whereby we MUST be saved"* (Acts 4:12).   None other is able to save. But Jesus is able to save to the uttermost all who "come unto God by Him, seeing He ever liveth to make intercession for them" (Heb. 7:25).   Christ, *who knew no sin,* was made to be sin *for us,* "that we might be made *the righteousness of God IN him"* (II Cor. 5:21).

2. *"MANY will say unto me in that day . . . ."*
In the language of Almighty God, what would be *"many"?* To me, a *thousand* people are "many people."   If I were riding down the road and I saw a flock of sheep or a herd of cattle with *five thousand* animals, that would certainly be "many." In our great tent meetings when we have from five thousand to seven or eight thousand people present, it seems to me that we have "many" people.   But would God consider it so?   When we think of the millions upon millions of people who have lived and died since Jesus spoke these words, I believe you will agree that what you and I con- sider "many" could be multiplied time without number in order to qualify as *"many"* in the sight of God.   And these "many" people are going to appear before God, exclaiming, "Lord, Lord...!"

3. *"Have we not PROPHESIED in thy name? and in thy name have CAST OUT DEVILS? and in thy name done many wonderful WORKS?"*
We think of a *prophet* as foretelling things which are yet to occur; but a prophet also *forthtells*

45

what has already been foretold. Therefore every minister, missionary, evangelist, pastor, or Bible teacher is a prophet in one sense of the word— i. e., they forthtell what has already been prophesied by holy men of God as they were moved by the Holy Ghost. Yet Jesus tells us that "many" of these will say to Him, "We have prophesied in your name"—and among the many will be hundreds of thousands of present-day liberals and modernists, men who profess to be Christian, yet deny the fundamentals of the faith. They declare that the virgin birth and the resurrection are but myths, and that the blood atonement is no longer necessary. They cry, "Lord, Lord!" even while denying the very thing for which Jesus died— *redemption through His BLOOD.* The sad thing is that these people are not *heathen.* They are men who prophesy *in the name of the Lord.*

There are tens of thousands of religionists in America who accept *Jesus Christ the SON* but deny God the Father and God the Holy Ghost as Persons in the Godhead. They say that Father, Son, and Holy Ghost are just titles—that Jesus is God, God is Jesus, and there is no such thing as the Trinity. They further say that this would constitute *three Gods.* Of course, there are *not* three Gods. There is *ONE God manifest in three Persons.* There are many who claim to be Christian yet teach and preach that there is *"Jesus ONLY,"* denying the Father and the Holy Spirit. Will

46

people who teach such error enter the kingdom of God? The only place to find the right answer is in the Word of God:

"Many deceivers are entered into the world, who confess not that Jesus Christ is come in the flesh. *This is a deceiver and an antichrist.* Look to yourselves, that we lose not those things which we have wrought, but that we receive a full reward. Whosoever transgresseth, and abideth not in the doctrine of Christ, hath not God. He that abideth in the doctrine of Christ, *he hath both THE FATHER AND THE SON.*

"If there come any unto you, and bring not this doctrine, *receive him not into your house, neither bid him God speed: for he that biddeth him God speed is PARTAKER OF HIS EVIL DEEDS"* (II John 7-11).

Read and re-read these verses. Study them, believe them. According to this passage, a person is evil who denies God the Father and God the Holy Ghost, outlawing them from the Trinity, and assuredly no evil person can enter heaven's glories! This Scripture emphatically tells us that if we deny the *doctrine* of Christ we do not *have* Christ. On the other hand, if we *accept* the doctrine of Christ we have *both the Father AND the Son.*

Matthew 3:16, 17 presents a perfect picture of the Holy Trinity. Jesus went to John the Baptist to be baptized of him in Jordan. "And *Jesus,* when He was baptized, went up straightway out of the water: and, lo, the heavens were opened unto Him, and He saw *the Spirit of God* descending like a dove, and lighting upon Him: and lo *a voice from heaven*, saying, This is my beloved Son, in whom I am well pleased."

Surely no reasonable person would deny the Trinity in this passage—God the Son standing in the water, God the Holy Ghost descending bodily in the form of a dove, and God the Father speaking from heaven, identifying His only begotten Son and placing His stamp of approval upon Him. *ONE God manifest in THREE PERSONS*—that is what the Bible definitely teaches. I do not *understand* the Holy Trinity, but I do not need to understand in order to believe it. "The just shall live by faith" (Rom. 1:17). If I could explain God, I would be as *wise* as God, and I am so thankful that my God is so much greater than I!

Not everyone who prophesies, preaches, or goes to the mission field is God's minister. Some of them are "false apostles, deceitful workers, transforming themselves into the apostles of Christ. And no marvel; for *Satan himself is transformed into an angel of light. Therefore it is no great thing if his ministers also be transformed as the ministers of righteousness;* whose end shall be according to their works" (II Cor. 11:13-15). Yes, the devil has *ministers*. They speak the language of the Bible—but they do not obey the truth they speak. They call Jesus *"Lord"*—but they do not do or preach the things He *commands* them to do and teach.

In Matthew 7:15 Jesus Himself warned of these false prophets. He said, *"Beware* of false prophets, which come to you in sheep's clothing, but inwardly they are *ravening wolves!"* Therefore, beloved, we must be careful which church we join and which ministers we support. There are many *false teachers* abroad in the land.

You may ask, "How can I *know* whether or not the minister I support is preaching the pure Word of God?" Let the Scripture answer: "Wherefore also it is contained in the Scripture, *Behold, I lay in Sion a chief corner stone, elect, precious: and he that believeth on Him SHALL NOT BE CONFOUNDED* (confused)" (I Pet. 2:6). Truly born again believers are not confused by the man in the pulpit. The Holy Spirit dwells within the heart of every believer (Rom. 8:9) and bears witness with our spirit that we are the children of God (Rom. 8:16). Therefore if you are born again you will recognize the Holy Spirit as He works through the man in the pulpit if that man be truly God's minister. You should get a good Bible and carry it to church with you. Then check on the man in the pulpit, and if he is not preaching the pure, unadulterated Word of God without fear or favor, do not support him with either your presence or your money!

The second thing these false prophets will say when they stand before God is, *"Lord, Lord, have we not . . . in thy name . . . cast out DEVILS?"* I can almost hear someone asking, "Mr. Greene, is it *possible* that an unconverted person could preach the Word of God, cast out demons, and have people saved under his preaching, even though he himself is not *born again?"* Yes, that *is* altogether possible. An unsaved Sunday school teacher can have people saved under his teaching. An evangelist can conduct revival and people be saved under his preaching although he himself is not a child of God. You see, it is not what the *man* is that leads people to be saved. It is *the Word of God* which he preaches. Certainly a man who is not born again cannot be a truly successful minister, missionary, or Bible teacher and have *a great number* of souls saved; but it is possible for *some* to accept Christ through the Word as it is read in their hearing. Remember, *"the Word of God is quick and powerful, and sharper than any twoedged sword, piercing even to the dividing asunder of soul and spirit, and of the joints and marrow, and is a discerner of the thoughts and intents of the heart"* (Heb. 4:12). The Word of God is *"the POWER of God unto salvation to every one that believeth"* (Rom. 1:16).

The Word of God is the incorruptible seed that brings the new birth (I Pet. 1:23). The Word brings faith (Rom. 10:17). Therefore, even though a *sinner* reads the Word in the presence of other sinners, it is not impossible for the Holy Spirit to take the Word and bear it home to the heart of the hearer. Yes, I shudder at this thought, but *there will be preachers in hell!*

It grieves me to make that statement. But any thinking person must admit that there are ministers today who claim to be God's men, yet deny the virgin birth, the blood atonement, the resurrection of Jesus. Oh, yes—they preach the Gospel after a fashion—that is, they read the Scriptures and then proceed to explain them away. But when the Word of God is read in the hearing of unbelievers, in some cases it will enter the ear and touch the heart! The entrance of the Word gives *light* (Psalm 119:130) and brings salvation.

"Many" will stand before Jesus and remind Him that in His name they have prophesied, cast out devils, and accomplished many wonderful works, and by reason of these things they expect to enter the kingdom of God. There are people today who think they are going to heaven because of the work they do in the local church, or because of the high moral life they live, or because of the money they give to the work of the Lord. There are men of means who give thousands of dollars to the building program of the church. They build chapels, they endow their denominational schools, they work hard to promote church membership and charitable enterprises. But what does the

Word of God say about these things?

In I Corinthians 13:1-3 the Apostle Paul explains that we may "speak with the tongues of men and of angels," we may "have the gift of prophecy," we may "understand all mysteries, and all knowledge," we may give all our earthly goods to feed the poor and give our bodies to be burned—but if we have not *charity* (love)—and *GOD is love*— all these other things will profit us *nothing!*

Dear friend, just because you have had an answer to prayer, just because you can teach a Sunday school class, give a good talk at prayer-meeting, or even preach a sermon, just because someone made a profession of faith at the close of one of your services, these things do not mean that you are born again. *Only they who do the WILL OF THE FATHER* are born again and sure for heaven!

What will Jesus say to the people who have done so many outstanding things in His name? The answer is found in our Scripture text—Matthew 7:23: "Then will I profess unto them, *I NEVER KNEW YOU! Depart from me, ye that work iniquity!*" Please underline and accept the words *"I never KNEW you."* These words were not spoken by some denominational preacher; they fell from the lips of the Son of God. He was not speaking to people who had been saved and then *lost* their salvation for one reason or another. These "many" were not once *IN grace* and then

OUT of grace. I am not trying to "indoctrinate" you. I am simply trying to point out that these people prophesied, cast out devils, and did wonderful works—but they were never, *never, NEVER* born again! Jesus in His own words declared, *"I NEVER knew you."*

It is possible for a person to make a tremendous outward show of religion, and yet never possess the Lord Jesus in the heart. Religions of *"works"* are growing by leaps and bounds the world over, because man wants some part in his own salvation. People want to *do* something, *give* something, *be* something—but *salvation is the GIFT OF GOD* and the only way to come into possession of a gift is to receive it from the giver. In John 1:12, 13 we read, "As many as *RECEIVED Him,* to them *gave He power* to become the sons of God, even to them that *believe on His name:* which were born, not of blood, nor of the will of the flesh, nor of the will of man, *BUT OF GOD."*

Titus 3:5 clearly explains that we are saved *"not* by works of righteousness which *we* have done, but *according to His MERCY He saved us,* by the washing of regeneration, and renewing of the Holy Ghost."

Ephesians 2:8, 9 declares, *"BY GRACE are ye saved through faith,* and that not of yourselves: *it is the GIFT OF GOD:* not of works, lest any man should boast."

Titus 2:11 tells us, *"The GRACE OF GOD that*

bringeth salvation hath appeared to all men."

So according to the clear, understandable teaching of the Bible, we are saved by GRACE—minus prophesying, minus casting out demons, minus wonderful works.

Could anything be sadder than for a person to expect to enter heaven, only to hear the Lord Jesus say, *"I never KNEW you! DEPART from me, ye that work iniquity"?* Like the guest without a wedding garment, he will hear the King say to His servants, *"Bind him hand and foot, and take him away, and cast him into outer darkness . . ."* (Matt. 22:13).

Dear reader, will you in all honesty ask yourself the solemn, eternal question, "Am I truly *born again?* Am I washed in the *blood?* Is my name written in the Lamb's book of life? or am I simply *practicing religion?*" Search your heart for the answer, and if you are born again, the Holy Spirit will witness with your spirit that you are a child of God (Rom. 8:16). If you do not have the witness of the Spirit, if you have not done the will of God, then I advise you to fall on your knees before an open Bible and stay there until you can say, *"Blessed assurance! Jesus is MINE!"* Do not be among the "many" who will stand before God expecting to spend eternity with Him—only to hear Him say, "Depart—I never knew you!" Could anything be more heartbreaking than the disappointment of missing heaven when you had *expected to go there?*

II
The Most Important Passage In the Bible

"There was a man of the Pharisees, named Nicodemus, a ruler of the Jews. The same came to Jesus by night, and said unto Him, Rabbi, we know that thou art a teacher come from God: for no man can do these miracles that thou doest, except God be with him.

"Jesus answered and said unto him, Verily, verily, I say unto thee, *Except a man be born again, he cannot see the kingdom of God.* Nicodemus saith unto Him, How can a man be born when he is old? Can he enter the second time into his mother's womb, and be born? Jesus answered, Verily, verily, I say unto thee, *Except a man be born of water and of the Spirit, he cannot enter into the kingdom of God.* That which is born of the flesh is flesh; and that which is born of the Spirit is spirit. Marvel not that I said unto thee, *Ye must be born again"* (John 3:1-7).

It is not imperative that you see this passage as I see it, but it *is* necessary that you believe and receive the truth of these verses if you hope to make heaven your home. That is why I call it *the most important* passage in the Bible.

"Verily, verily, I say unto thee, *EXCEPT a man be BORN AGAIN, he cannot see the kingdom of God."* These words were not spoken by some fanatical, narrow-minded pastor or evangelist. They fell from the lips of the Son of God—and they are *truth*. It is imperative that a person be born again if he hopes to see or enter the kingdom of God.

Let us look briefly at the man to whom these words were addressed: His name was Nicodemus, and he was a Pharisee—which means that he was a religious man. The Pharisees were very strict in their religious practices. Nicodemus was a ruler in the synagogue—Jesus called him "a master of Israel" (John 3:10). He was no ordinary man. He was religious, respected, refined, well educated, and he held a position of importance in the nation Israel.

Furthermore, this man was no hypocrite. You will notice that not once in His conversation with Nicodemus did Jesus even remotely suggest that hypocrisy was involved. Here was a sincere seeker of truth, and Jesus knew the heart of Nicodemus, as He knows the hearts of all of us today.

This man "came to Jesus *by night*." It has been suggested that Nicodemus sought the Lord by night because he was *ashamed to be seen* going to talk with Him and chose the night time rather than going to Him in the daylight hours. I disagree with that interpretation. I think the reason Nicodemus went to Jesus by night was simply that he was so busy with his religious activities during the day, he did not have *time* to seek the

Lord during daylight hours.

This is true of many religionists today. They are so busy trying to keep their religious machinery running, so busy serving the ecclesiastical dictators, that they have no time to get saved! Even among born again Christians we find many who are so busy with religious activities in one form or another that they do not have time to witness and win souls. They are occupied with the "program."

Nicodemus confessed that he knew Jesus was a teacher from God. His miracles testified that He was God's Man, and Nicodemus knew enough about God to know that the things Jesus was doing were not the works of an ordinary man. This ruler in Israel had a hunger in his heart. He was religious—but religion did not satisfy. He was a master in Israel—but his office and learning did not satisfy the longing of his soul. He heard about this great Teacher, heard about His miracles, heard about His wonderful words of life. So he sought Him out—and Jesus never turned a deaf ear to any man's plea if that man was sincerely seeking the things of God.

When Nicodemus acknowledged Jesus as a teacher come from God, He replied, "Except a man (*any* man, *all* men, even *you, Nicodemus*) be born again, he cannot see the kingdom of God." In other words, "Nicodemus, you are a religious man, you are an educated man, and you have a position of authority among the religious leaders of Israel. So it is not *'religion'* that you need, it is not *teaching* that you need. *You need to be BORN AGAIN!"*

As a teacher in Israel, this man knew the prophecies in Isaiah chapter 53, prophecies dealing with the coming of Messiah. He *knew* the Old Testament Scriptures, but he did not *understand* them. A learned man in religion, he did not need *teaching* as much as he needed *enlightenment.* In other words, he needed to *obey* the teaching he already had!

It is evident that Nicodemus was thinking in terms of the natural rather than the spiritual. He asked, "How *can* a man be born when he is *old?* Can he enter the second time into his mother's womb, and be born?" There was no sarcasm here. Nicodemus was sincere, he was seeking the answer to what seemed to him an impossibility. Jesus recognized the sincerity of his question and explained, "That which is born of the flesh is *flesh;* that which is born of the Spirit is *spirit."* In spite of his learning and his religious training, Nicodemus had never grasped the meaning of the miracle of God, the supernatural power to give a *spiritual* birth to people, even when they are "old."

Like Nicodemus, most religions go no further than the realm of the natural. Religions of works, religions of "do's" and "don't's," are spreading over the world like wildfire today. The masses want to "see something," or "feel something." They are not willing to accept the gift of God—salvation by grace through faith in the finished work of the Lord Jesus Christ. The pure religion of Christianity is not reaching the masses.

Step by gentle step Jesus led Nicodemus into the light of salvation, the miracle of the new birth. He spoke to him of the movement of the *wind*—"the wind bloweth where it listeth, and thou hearest the sound thereof, but canst not tell whence it cometh, and whither it goeth. *So is every one that is born of the Spirit"* (John 3:8). We do not understand the wind—we do not know where it comes from nor whither it goes; but *we accept the FACT of the wind.* So it is with the new birth. We do not have to understand it to accept it as *fact.*

Jesus further explained to Nicodemus with the illustration of the serpent in the wilderness—a fact with which this teacher in Israel would certainly have been familiar. He said, *"As Moses lifted up the serpent in the wilderness, even so must the Son of man be lifted up:* that whosoever believeth in Him should not perish, but have eternal life" (John 3:14, 15).

This brought light to the soul of Nicodemus. He knew the history of his own people, and he understood the reference to the brazen serpent lifted up in the wilderness, when fiery serpents had bitten the Israelites. The only requirement was that they *"look—and LIVE."* Those who looked upon the brazen serpent *lived.* Those who *refused* to look *died.* So the power of the Gospel— yes, the *Old Testament Gospel*—brought light to the heart of Nicodemus. He saw it, he believed it—and if he was not saved that very night he certainly became a learner of truth and was saved at a later date. Personally, I believe he was born again at the time of his conversation with Jesus. It was Nicodemus who later defended his Lord before the Pharisees by asking them, "Doth our law judge any man, before it hear him, and know what he doeth?" (John 7:51). It was also Nicodemus who came with Joseph of Arimathaea and asked Pilate for the dead body of the crucified Christ, that they might prepare it for burial and lay it in Joseph's new tomb "wherein was never man yet laid" (John 19:38-41). Yes, I believe Nicodemus was saved that night, and I expect to meet him in Paradise one glorious day!

"Marvel not that I said unto *thee, YE must be born again"* (John 3:7). Nicodemus undoubtedly showed his perplexity. Perhaps he displayed a look of astonishment when Jesus told him the absolute, divine necessity to be born again if he would enter the kingdom of God. He was clean in his manner of life. He was honest and upright in character. He was religious and respectable. Was it possible that he needed something more than this in order to enter heaven? Perhaps it was such thoughts as these that caused Jesus to say to him, "Marvel not, Nicodemus; for no matter how morally clean a man's life may be, *ALL men, EVERY man, MUST be born again* in order to enter the kingdom."

In John 1:12, 13 we are told, "As many as received Him, to them gave He power to become the sons of God, even to them that believe on His name: which were born—not of blood, nor of the will of the flesh, nor of the will of man, but of God." These are tremendous verses. There is enough Gospel in this passage to save the entire world *if the world would only believe the TRUTH of the passage.* We are saved by receiving Jesus. Notice *"as MANY as received Him"* takes in everyone and excludes no one. Then we also notice that to those who receive Jesus, *God GIVES the power* of the new birth. Man cannot earn or merit the power to become a child of God, nor can that power be bought. The new birth comes through the miraculous power of Almighty God, and He furnishes that power when we believe on the Lord Jesus Christ.

We are born into God's family—"not of *blood,* nor of the will of the *flesh,* nor of the *will of man.*" Many people are proud of their *blood lines.* They have generations of illustrious ancestors behind them, they are of aristocratic heritage. But no matter how upright, aristocratic, or even *godly* one's ancestral blood lines may be, neither that

61

blood nor that flesh can help to "born" the natural man into the kingdom of God!

Neither are we born again *of the WILL of man.* No man has ever been willing for God to tell him what to do—that is, not until he has been born again. Noah, Moses, and Abraham were all three outstanding men of God. They were giants in God's service. *But they all sinned!* There came a time when each of them rebelled against God. Certainly *no natural man* is willing to follow God's directions until God puts a new will (His *own* will) into the heart of man, through the new birth.

Man is by nature a child of wrath (Eph. 2:3), totally depraved. But when we are born into heaven's family we have a *new* nature: "Whereby are given unto us exceeding great and precious promises: that by these ye might be *partakers of the DIVINE nature,* having escaped the corruption that is in the world through lust" (II Pet. 1:4). *"THEREFORE—if any man be IN CHRIST, he is a NEW creature: old things are passed away; behold, ALL things are become new"* (II Cor. 5:17).

What I am trying to drive home to your heart is this: *You MUST be born again if you hope to enter heaven.* Always keep in mind that what God demands, God provides. Whatever He requires of you, He makes it possible for you to do. The new birth, *God's MUST,* is provided by Him, and His Word emphatically declares, *"Therefore thou art INEXCUSABLE, O man!"* (Rom. 2:1).

I have called this the most important passage in the Word of God, because it gives God's divine imperative of redemption—*"EXCEPT a man be born again, he cannot see the kingdom of God!"* Have *you* been born again? Do you know beyond any shadow of doubt that you are a child of God? If you do not know that you are saved as surely as you know that you are breathing, I urge you to go on your knees before God and tell Him that you repent of your sins, and ask Him to save you. He will save you this moment, and you will know it!

III
The Most Glorious Passage In the Bible

"That which was from the beginning, which we have heard, which we have seen with our eyes, which we have looked upon, and our hands have handled, of the Word of life; (for the life was manifested, and we have seen it, and bear witness, and shew unto you that eternal life, which was with the Father, and was manifested unto us). That which we have seen and heard declare we unto you, that ye also may have fellowship with us: and truly our fellowship is with the Father, and with His Son Jesus Christ. And these things write we unto you, that your joy may be full.

"This then is the message which we have heard of Him, and declare unto you, that God is light, and in Him is no darkness at all. If we say that we have fellowship with Him, and walk in darkness, we lie, and do not the truth: but if we walk in the light, as He is in the light, we have fellowship one with another, and *the blood of Jesus Christ His Son cleanseth us from all sin"* (I John 1:1-7).

The last verse in this passage is a most glorious verse: "If we walk in the light, as He is in the light, we have fellowship one with another, *and THE BLOOD OF JESUS CHRIST HIS SON cleanseth us from ALL sin!"* Beloved, do you know anything that could be *more wonderful, more soul-satisfying, more GLORIOUS,* than to know that every sin—all *trace* of sin—has been washed away in the precious blood of the Lord Jesus Christ?

The blood of Jesus—and *ONLY the blood of Jesus*—satisfies God. In I Peter 1:18, 19 we read, "Forasmuch as ye know that ye were not redeemed with corruptible things, as silver and gold, from your vain conversation received by tradition from your fathers, *but with THE PRECIOUS BLOOD OF CHRIST, as of a lamb without blemish and without spot."* So we are not redeemed with *"corruptible* things." This assures us that redemption does not come by anything man can do! Man cannot save himself, nor can he *assist God* in the saving. Man has corrupted everything he has ever touched. The human heart is "deceitful above all things, and desperately wicked. Who can know it?'' (Jer. 17:9). Let us face it, beloved: Apart from God, man is hopeless, helpless, and hell-bound—and only the applied blood of the Lord Jesus Christ can make one fit for heaven.

Yet one of the hardest things for any of God's preachers to do is to get sinners to step aside and leave self out of God's plan of salvation, and let God save them. It is the nature of unregenerate man to want to *do* something, *be* something, or *give* something. He wants to feel that he, himself, has a part in his salvation. Every religion of "works" known in this world today—and they are without number—is based on the idea that man must contribute something or provide something in order to be saved; and every such cult or religion was founded by man.

Now it is true that "faith without works is dead" (James 2:20), and while saving faith *produces works, WORKS will never produce SAVING FAITH*. We are not saved by "works of righteousness which we have done," but according to God's *mercy*, "by the washing of regeneration, and renewing of the Holy Ghost, which He shed on us abundantly *through Jesus Christ our Saviour*" (Tit. 3:5, 6).

There are outstanding religionists today who refer to the ministers of the true Gospel as preaching a "butcherhouse theology and a bloody God." I would remind these religionists that according to the Word of God, *"without shedding of BLOOD*

is no remission'' (Heb. 9:22). The blood began to
flow in the Garden of Eden when Adam and Eve
disobeyed God and then attempted to cover their
sin by the work of their own hands. God condemned their *bloodless covering* and Himself provided coats of skins—at the expense of the blood
of innocent animals. From that day unto this day
in which we live, God has demanded blood atonement—but it was a *sinless* Substitute who must
pay the sin-debt. Therefore, I repeat, what God
demands, God *provides.* In His only begotten
Son, sinless Lamb of God, He provided the blood-
covering for sin.

In Luke 22:19, 20 when Jesus instituted the Lord's
Supper, "He took bread, and gave thanks, and
brake it, and gave unto them, saying, This is my
body which is given for you: this do in remem-
brance of me. Likewise also the cup after supper,
saying, *This cup is the new testament in MY
BLOOD, WHICH IS SHED FOR YOU."* When
we partake of the Lord's Supper today, we are
giving testimony that His body was broken and
His blood was shed for the remission of sin. God
Almighty demands blood; and regardless of what
religionists may teach or preach, sinful man will
be covered by the blood of Jesus or he will burn
in hell, for *without* shedding of blood there is no
remission of sin. There is no saving power outside
the power of the blood of Jesus.

The Apostle Paul was a blood-preacher. Let us

hear what he said to the believers in Rome concerning redemption through the blood:

"But now the righteousness of God without the law is manifested, being witnessed by the law and the prophets; even the righteousness of God which is by faith of Jesus Christ unto all and upon all them that believe: for there is no difference: for all have sinned, and come short of the glory of God; being justified freely by His grace through the redemption that is in Christ Jesus: Whom God hath set forth to be a propitiation through faith in His blood, to declare His righteousness for the remission of sins that are past, through the forbearance of God; to declare, I say, at this time His righteousness: that He might be just, and the Justifier of him which believeth in Jesus.

"Where is boasting then? It is excluded. By what law? of works? Nay: but by the law of faith. Therefore we conclude that a man is justified by faith without the deeds of the law" (Rom. 3:21-28).

Notice especially verse 25 in this passage: God set Jesus forth "to be a propitiation *through faith in HIS BLOOD*"—not through faith in His sinless life, not through faith in His great miracles, not through faith in the great example He set. Salvation is *through faith in the blood of Jesus.* No blood, no salvation. If you are a believer and you are attending a church where a bloodless gospel is preached, you should get out of that church and

Behold the Man!

lend your presence and your support in a church where God's man believes and preaches *the blood atonement.* If you are supporting a minister who does not preach salvation through faith in Jesus and the blood atonement, you are supporting a minister of the devil—and just in case you do not fully appreciate that statement please read II Corinthians 11:13-15 and II John, verses 7-11. Give your full attention to those two passages and see what the holy Scriptures say about ministers of Satan, and about the danger in supporting such a man!

There is *no redemption apart from the blood of Jesus*—"in whom we have *REDEMPTION THROUGH HIS BLOOD, even the forgiveness of sins"* (Col. 1:14). Let me point out seven steps in what the precious blood of Christ has done, is doing, and will do for us:

1. The blood stays the judgment hand of Almighty God.

Just as the blood of the paschal lamb averted judgment on the night of the Passover in Egypt (Ex. 12:13) the blood of Jesus averts the judgment of God against sin today. "Christ our passover is sacrificed for us" (I Cor. 5:7), and when believers stand before God *the verdict will STILL BE, "When I see the BLOOD, I will pass over you!"*

2. The blood converts the one who believes in Christ.

The blood of cleansing changed the position

68

and condition of the cleansed leper (Lev. 14:14). Leprosy is a type of sin, and unregenerate man is a spiritual leper until he is cleansed by the precious blood of Christ, our Substitute who "loved us, and washed us from our sins in His own blood" (Rev. 1:5).

3. The blood inverts the position we once occupied.

Instead of being *IN the world,* believers are separated *FROM the world.* God said to Pharaoh, "I will put a division *(redemption)* between my people and thy people" (Ex. 8:23). The blood of Jesus puts a division (redemption) between us and the world. When we are covered by the blood, "the world knoweth us not, *because it knew HIM not"* (I John 3:1).

4. The blood inserts us in a new place.

The blood of the covenant enabled Moses and the seventy elders to draw near to the God of Israel (Ex. 24:5-10). So the blood of Jesus enables us to draw near to God. It inserts us into a new realm. "Our conversation (citizenship) is *in heaven,* from whence also we look for the Saviour, the Lord Jesus Christ" (Phil. 3:20). "God, who is rich in mercy, for His great love wherewith He loved us . . . hath raised us up together, and made us sit together *in heavenly places in Christ Jesus"* (Eph. 2:4, 6). Believers are *"hid with Christ IN God"* (Col. 3:3). Glorious position! Amen!

5. The blood asserts blessings to the believer.

The blessing of *peace* is ours through the blood. Jesus "made peace through the blood of His cross, by Him to reconcile *ALL things* unto Himself . . . whether they be things in earth, or things in heaven" (Col. 1:20).

The blessing of *pardon* is ours. We have redemption through the blood of Jesus, "the forgiveness of sins, according to the riches of His grace" (Eph. 1:7).

The blessing of *victory* is ours. Through the blood of Jesus we have the power to overcome anything hell may hurl at us: "And they overcame him by the blood of the Lamb, and by the word of their testimony . . ." (Rev. 12:11).

The blessing of *cleansing* is ours. Through the blood of Jesus we are made holy and pure. "The blood of Jesus Christ (God's) Son cleanseth us *from ALL sin*" (I John 1:7).

The blessing of *Paradise* is ours. The blood of Jesus asserts that all who have washed their robes in the blood of the Lamb are *guaranteed Paradise* on the other side: "After this I beheld, and, lo, a great multitude which no man could number, of all nations, and kindreds, and people, and tongues, stood before the throne, and before the Lamb, clothed with white robes, and palms in their hands. . . . These are they which came out of great tribulation, *and have washed their robes, and made them white in the blood of the Lamb*" (Rev. 7:9, 14).

Hallelujah! for the blood that pardons, brings peace, gives power, secures purity, and guarantees Paradise! Are *you* under the blood?

6. *The blood exerts a powerful influence.*

The powerful influence of the blood has a practical bearing on our daily lives. In the first place, *it kills sin:* "Likewise reckon ye also yourselves to be *DEAD indeed unto sin,* but alive unto God through Jesus Christ our Lord. Let not sin therefore reign in your mortal body, that ye should obey it in the lusts thereof" (Rom. 6:11, 12).

In the second place, the blood of Jesus *slays self* and removes selfishness from the heart: "For the love of Christ constraineth us; because we thus judge, that if one died for all, then were all dead; and that He died for all, that they which live *should not henceforth live unto THEMSELVES, but unto Him which died for them,* and rose again" (II Cor. 5:14, 15).

In the third place, the blood of Jesus helps us to *overcome pride:* "Let this mind be in you, which was also in Christ Jesus: who, being in the form of God, thought it not robbery to be equal with God; but made Himself *of no reputation,* and took upon Him *the form of a servant,* and was made in the likeness of men: and being found in fashion as a man, *He humbled Himself, and became obedient unto death, even the death of the cross*" (Phil. 2:5-8). There is no room for pride in the heart of the believer.

71

7. The blood subverts the powers of hell.

"Fear not! I am the first and the last. I am He that liveth, and was dead; and, behold, I am alive for evermore, Amen; *and have the KEYS of HELL and of death*" (Rev. 1:17,18). Through Christ's death on the cross and His shed blood, all the powers of hell were defeated and conquered, and He now holds the keys of death and hell. Christians do not fear death or hell because our Saviour holds the keys—He purchased them with His own shed blood. He fought and conquered principalities and powers and rulers of spiritual wickedness in high places; and He ever lives to make intercession for us. Therefore we can say, "In *all these things* we are *MORE than conquerors* through Him that loved us" (Rom. 8:37).

God demands holiness and purity. The blood of Jesus *provides* holiness and purity for those who have been *washed* in His blood, for "the blood of Jesus Christ, (God's) Son, *cleanseth us from ALL sin.*" Is it any wonder that this seems to me to be the most *glorious* passage in God's holy Word? Cleansed from sin and made fit for heaven! What could be *more* glorious?

Are *your* sins under the blood? Have *you* been to Jesus for the cleansing power? If so, that is glorious. But if you are *not* saved, if you have not been cleansed from sin by the blood of Jesus, I urge you to read the following Scriptures—and then take God at His word:

"For God so loved the world, that He gave His only begotten Son, that *WHOSOEVER believeth in Him* should not perish, but have everlasting life. For God sent not His Son into the world to condemn the world; but that the world through Him might be saved. He that believeth on Him is not condemned: but *he that believeth NOT is condemned ALREADY,* because he hath not believed in the name of the only begotten Son of God" (John 3:16-18).

"For by grace are ye saved through faith; and that not of yourselves: it is the gift of God: not of works, lest any man should boast" (Eph. 2:8, 9).

"If thou shalt confess with thy mouth the Lord Jesus, and shalt believe in thine heart that God hath raised Him from the dead, thou shalt be saved. For with the heart man believeth unto righteousness: and with the mouth confession is made unto salvation. . . . For whosoever shall call upon the name of the Lord shall be saved" (Rom. 10:9, 10, 13).

Read these Scriptures, believe what God says in them, and call on Jesus to save you. He will do it, and you will know it!

The God of Reason

The God of Reason

"Come now, and let us reason together, saith the Lord: Though your sins be as scarlet, they shall be as white as snow; though they be red like crimson, they shall be as wool" (Isa. 1:18).

The great God of this universe, with all of His interests and activities, still has time to reason with each and every one of us if we will only let Him.   What a shame that so many of His creatures have no time for Him at all!   Yet a careful study of the Word of God reveals that the most sensible thing any human being can do is to hear the call of God, listen to His reasoning, trust Him and serve Him.

Why should we come to God and allow Him to reason with us?   There are many reasons.   We will look at only a few:

1. God commands us to come to Him.

"Come NOW!"   This is a direct command from God's Word that we come to Him and let Him reason with us.   And why should we obey a command from a God we have never seen, just because the Bible *tells* us to come to Him?   We should obey because we owe *our everything* to Him.   He is directly responsible for everything

77

we have, and for everything that we are.

God created the universe in which we live. "In the beginning God created the heaven and the earth" (Gen. 1:1). Even if man had evolved from nothing and nowhere, where would the human race live if God had not created the dirt on which we walk?

Not only did God create the universe and this earth on which man lives, he also *created MAN.* "God said, Let us make man in our image, after our likeness: and let them have dominion over the fish of the sea, and over the fowl of the air, and over the cattle, and over all the earth, and over every creeping thing that creepeth upon the earth. *So God created man in His own image, in the image of God created He him;* male and female created He them" (Gen. 1:26, 27). We owe our *existence* to the God who commands us to come to Him and allow Him to reason with us.

Not only did God create man as well as the earth on which man lives, He has given us every good thing that has ever come our way. *"Every* good gift and *every* perfect gift is from above, and cometh down from the Father of lights, with whom is no variableness, neither shadow of turning" (James 1:17). *EVERY good and perfect gift* — good things beyond number, and they all come directly from God! For example, dear reader, your *brain* is a gift from God — you *could* have been an idiot! Your *nationality* is a gift from God — you could have been born in the jungle! What *health* you have is a gift from God—even your *job* is a gift from God, for there are millions of people who do not have a job and a chance to earn a good living. Consider your wife or husband, your children, the clothes you wear, the car you drive, the food you eat, your home—and the everyday things so taken for granted, such as the sunshine and rain.

All these things—and many, many more—are from God. If the devil had *his* way, you would not be reading this sermon. He would have killed you a long time ago and you would be in hell today, begging for a drop of water! Therefore, since God created the earth on which you live, and since He has given you every good thing in your life, does He not have a right to ask you to serve Him? Does He not have a right to *command* you to come to Him and let Him reason with you? Indeed *He does!*

2. *God is the only One who can keep us out of hell.*

Only the God who created us can keep us out of hell and make reservations for us to spend eternity in heaven with Him. "For God so loved the world, that He gave His only begotten Son, that whosoever believeth in Him should not perish, but have everlasting life" (John 3:16). God's love and grace provided our redemption. It was Jesus who left the glories of heaven to come into the world and die for us—but it was God the Father *who so LOVED* us that He *gave* His only Son, set Him forth to be a propitiation for our sins—"and not for our's only, but also for the sins of the whole world" (I John 2:2).

When Adam sinned in the Garden of Eden, God promised a Redeemer, the seed of the woman, who would bruise the serpent's head (Gen. 3:15). That promise was fulfilled when God sent His Son into the world to die for sinners such as you and I.

Men in the past have made their own gods—and the same is true today. They may not make idols of gold, silver, or wood—but there are thousands of religionists who are following their own ideas and making their own rules in religious practices. But beloved, there is *only ONE way* to reach heaven and the Paradise of God, and that is *GOD'S way*. "There is a way that *seemeth* right unto a man, *but the END thereof are the ways of DEATH*" (Prov. 16:25).

The Lord Jesus Christ is the only Person who ever satisfied the great heart of God. He never once disobeyed the Father's wish. He declared, ". . . I do *always* those things that please Him" (John 8:29). To His disciples He said, "My meat is to do the will of Him that sent me, and to finish His work" (John 4:34). Just before He went to the cross He said to the heavenly Father, "I have *finished the work* which thou gavest me to do" (John 17:4), and *from the cross* He cried out to the whole world, *"It is FINISHED!"* and gave His spirit back into the hands of God (John 19:30; Luke 23:46).

Therefore the only way man can satisfy God is in God's only begotten Son, the Lord Jesus Christ. Three times during Christ's earthly ministry God spoke from heaven, acknowledging His approval of Jesus (Matt. 3:17; 17:5; John 12:28). No such announcement has ever come from heaven concerning any other person who has ever lived on this earth! I repeat: There is *only ONE WAY* to reach heaven, and that is God's way.

God's way is the *Jesus* way.

The Jesus way is the *blood* way.

The blood way is the *cross* way.

In spite of all that the liberals and modernists have said and are saying about the cross of Jesus and the blood-bought salvation, the Bible still declares, *"WITHOUT shedding of blood is NO REMISSION!"* (Heb. 9:22). Beloved, if you are not a born again child of God, I urge you to obey His command to come to Him and let Him reason with you concerning your soul. He is the only One who can keep you out of a devil's hell and give you a home in heaven.

3. God's gift is free for the asking.

The most reasonable thing a person can do is come to God and trust His Christ *because*—He has made all things ready, and His unspeakable gift is *free.* God's only begotten Son *purchased* our salvation at the cost of His own life and His shed blood. Eternal life is ours for the taking, through faith in the finished work of Jesus.

If it were necessary for man to reach certain standards before being eligible for salvation, I am afraid most of us would be left out! If it were necessary to have a required amount of money in the bank, or live in a given section of the country, or have diplomas from high school and college, or have a certain color of skin, or reach a given moral standard—all before we could be saved—then most of us would never be eligible to receive God's great salvation. But such is not the case. The only requirement we must meet before we can have an audience with God is simply to obey His command and come to Him! So dear friend, if you have a desire to receive the blessings of God upon your life, if you *want* to come into the family of heaven, all you need do is come to Him—*and the two of you "reason together."*

If you believe there is a heaven and a hell—

If you want to go to heaven and stay out of hell—

If you want the blessings of God upon your life—

If you want the Lord Jesus to come into your heart—

Your *only requirement* is that you *come* to God. As the precious old song so truthfully declares:

> *Just as I am, without one plea,*
> *But that thy blood was shed for me,*
> *And that thou bidst me come to thee —*
> *O Lamb of God — I COME!*

And what must you do when you come to Him? What is your part in salvation? If you accept the answers of preachers and religionists on that subject you will be thoroughly confused, because they do not agree. But the Bible has a plain answer, and the Bible answer can be trusted:

"Believe on the Lord Jesus Christ, and thou shalt be saved" (Acts 16:31). This is the answer Paul and Silas gave the Philippian jailer when he asked, "Sirs, *what must I do* to be saved?" To believe in Jesus is to believe that He *is,* and that He is everything the Bible *says* He is.

Do *you* believe that Jesus came into the world and died for sinners?

Do you believe that wicked hands nailed Him to a Roman cross and that He bled and died there?

Do you believe that He was buried, and on the third day rose from the dead?

If you can answer *"Yes"* to these questions, you are at the door of salvation and all you need do is step in:

"If thou shalt confess with thy mouth the Lord Jesus, and shalt believe in thine heart that God hath raised Him from the dead, *thou shalt be SAVED.* For with the heart man believeth unto righteousness; and with the mouth confession is made unto salvation" (Rom. 10:9, 10).

These are the verses that brought me to the Lord and gave me the assurance of my salvation. The passage is very clear and easily understood— *with the mouth* confess Jesus as Lord, and *with the heart* believe that God raised Him from the dead. Then a miracle takes place, God's miracle of the new birth!

To believe on Jesus unto salvation is to believe that He is the Jesus whom God sent into the world to die for sinners. To believe on Jesus unto salvation is to believe that He loved sinners so much that He willingly came into the world to do the Father's will and die on the cross in our stead. So, dear unsaved friend, if you believe that Jesus loves you and wants to save you, if you believe that He is *able* to save you, you are ready for salvation! Receive Jesus into your heart and the work is done.

4. God has made complete provision for our victory.

God not only loved us so much that He purchased our salvation with the precious blood of His only begotten Son, He loves us so much that He has made provision for our victory over the power of sin in this life, and final victory over even the *presence* of sin when we go to be with Him for all eternity! God does not save us—and then leave us to fight our own battles against the wiles of the devil, against the spiritual wickedness of this world. No indeed! He provides our every need for every trial and temptation we will ever be called upon to face while we live in this sin-cursed world:

"There hath no temptation taken you but such as is common to man: but *God is faithful,* who will not suffer you to be tempted above that ye are able; but will with the temptation also make *a way to escape,* that ye may be able to bear it" (I Cor. 10:13).

When God saves us by grace through faith, He does not leave us unidentified; He places a seal of ownership at the door of our heart—He seals us with the Holy Spirit (Eph. 4:30) "which is the earnest of our inheritance until the redemption of the purchased possession, unto the praise of His glory" (Eph. 1:14). Never forget that the devil knows to whom the Christian belongs—and he also knows that Jesus is his Master! There will be temptations, there will be trials and tribulations; but God knew all of this when He blueprinted the plan of salvation, and He made provision for it in the giving of His Son. Jesus said to His disciples, *"In the world ye shall have tribulation: but be of good cheer; I HAVE OVERCOME THE WORLD"* (John 16:33). Therefore, *IN HIM we are MORE than conquerors* (Rom. 8:37).

5. God has provided for our physical needs.

When God commanded us to come to Him, He left *absolutely no need* for which He has not made provision. Not only did He provide free salvation, and a way of escape from and victory over temptation, but He also made provision for every *physical need* as well.

If you will study the life of Jesus as He walked on earth you will find that He was concerned about the welfare of His followers. He provided food when they had toiled all night at their nets and had taken no fish (John 21:3-14). He provided money to pay Peter's taxes to keep down criticism (Matt. 17:24-27). He provided clothes for the naked man of Gadara (Mark 5:15; Luke 8:35).

Not only is God *able* to supply our needs, He also *promises* to do so. In Matthew 6:25-33 Jesus said, "Take no thought for your life, what ye shall eat, or what ye shall drink; nor yet for your body, what ye shall put on. Is not the life more than meat, and the body than raiment? Behold the fowls of the air: for they sow not, neither do they reap, nor gather into barns; yet *your heavenly Father feedeth them. Are ye not much better than they?* . . . And why take ye thought for raiment? Consider the lilies of the field, how they grow; they toil not, neither do they spin: and yet I say unto you, That even Solomon in all his glory was not arrayed like one of these.

"Wherefore, if God so clothe the grass of the field, which to day is, and to morrow is cast into the oven, *shall He not much more clothe YOU, O ye of little faith?* Therefore take no thought, saying, What shall we eat? or, What shall we drink? or, Wherewithal shall we be clothed? . . . for your heavenly Father knoweth that ye have need of all these things. *But seek ye FIRST the kingdom of God, and His righteousness; and ALL THESE THINGS SHALL BE ADDED UNTO YOU!"*

In Psalm 84:11 we find this precious promise: "The Lord God is a sun and shield: the Lord will give grace and glory: *NO GOOD THING will He withhold from them that walk uprightly!"*

David testified, "I have been young, and now am old; *yet have I not seen the righteous forsaken, nor his seed begging bread"* (Psalm 37:25).

The Apostle Paul instructed the believers at Philippi, "Be careful for nothing; but in every thing by prayer and supplication with thanksgiving *let your requests be made known UNTO GOD"* (Phil. 4:6).

And finally, also testified by the Apostle Paul, we read, *"My God shall supply ALL YOUR NEED according to His riches in glory BY CHRIST JESUS"* (Phil. 4:19).

Who could ask for *more?* Is our God not a God of reason? Has He not provided a reasonable salvation? And is it not reasonable that we should obey His command to come to Him and allow Him to reason with us? He gave us this earth to be our home, He created us in His own image, He is the Giver of every good and perfect gift.

Furthermore, He so loved us that He gave Jesus to die for us, that through faith in His finished work we might be made fit for heaven. He also provided protection for His children every step of the way to heaven. He provided a storehouse of provisions—spiritual, physical, financial—whatsoever the child of God needs, in this life and in the life to come, God provided in His beloved Son, the Lord Jesus Christ.

6. *God has provided for our eternal needs.*

"Let not your heart be troubled: ye believe in God, believe also in me. In my Father's house are many mansions: if it were not so, I would have told you. *I go to prepare a place for YOU.* And if I go and prepare a place for you, *I WILL COME AGAIN, and receive you unto myself; that where I am, there ye may be also*" (John 14:1-3).

Jesus left this earth more than nineteen hundred years ago, to prepare an eternal home for all who accept Him as Saviour. Now when we consider that God made this earth and everything in it in *six days,* and He has been working on our future home for more than *nineteen centuries,* we cannot but wonder at the beauty that home will display! And it is in that home that God will display "the exceeding riches of His grace in His kindness toward us through Christ Jesus" throughout the endless ages of eternity (Eph. 2:6, 7).

In addition to our heavenly home, God will give us a *body* to *match* that home. Heaven will be a glory world, and we will need a body of glory in order to live there. God has made provision for that, and in I John 3:1, 2 we are told, "Behold, what manner of love the Father hath bestowed upon us, that we should be called the sons of God: therefore the world knoweth us not, because it knew Him not. Beloved, *NOW are we the sons of God,* and it doth not yet appear what we shall be: but *we know that, when He shall appear, we shall be LIKE HIM,* for we shall see Him as He is!"

Hallelujah! Who could possibly bring any accusation against, or find fault with, a God who created the universe in which we live—and could blow it up this second if He so desired? Who would dare reject or ignore a God who created man in His own image, breathed into his nostrils the breath of life—and could, if He chose, annihilate man from the earth this very moment?

How could anyone refuse to obey a God who loved sinners so much that He provided salvation for sinful man at the awful cost of the life's blood of His only begotten Son, sending Jesus into the world to die for sinners that sinners might be made fit for the kingdom of heaven?

God gave the most precious treasure heaven had, and then turned His head while wicked men nailed Jesus to the cross. God did not intervene at Calvary because He loved us so much He wanted to provide salvation for us and have us with Him through all eternity! He will go with every child of

His *all the way* through this life, and on through the valley of the shadow of death—and then He will greet us at the door of Paradise! Every provision was made for us in the Lord Jesus Christ, and all of this is ours *through Him.*

What could be unreasonable about asking any man to come to our God? I call heaven, earth, hell, angels, and man to the witness stand, and in the words of Pilate I ask, *"What accusation bring ye against this God?"*

Did you say, "None whatsoever!" Is that what you said? Then I ask you, *Are you serving Him with all your heart?* Have you surrendered heart, soul, spirit, and body to Him? If not, then it is evident that there is something wrong with Him insofar as *you* are concerned!

Dear sinner, hear the voice of God calling, "Come now, and let us reason together! Though your sins be as scarlet, they shall be as white as snow. Though they be red like crimson, they shall be as wool." Won't you bow your head right now and let God reason with you? Let Jesus speak peace to your troubled soul. Come to Him, tell Him that you have sinned against Him and ask Him to forgive you and save your soul. He will hear your cry and save you this moment.

If you are a *Christian,* dear reader, the most reasonable thing you have ever done was to come to the great God of reason and redemption.

Except Ye Repent!

Except Ye Repent!

"There were present at that season some that told Him of the Galilaeans, whose blood Pilate had mingled with their sacrifices. And Jesus answering said unto them, Suppose ye that these Galilaeans were sinners above all the Galilaeans, because they suffered such things? I tell you, Nay: but, except ye repent, ye shall all likewise perish. Or those eighteen, upon whom the tower in Siloam fell, and slew them, think ye that they were sinners above all men that dwelt in Jerusalem? I tell you, Nay: but, except ye repent, ye shall all likewise perish.

"He spake also this parable: A certain man had a fig tree planted in his vineyard; and he came and sought fruit thereon, and found none. Then said he unto the dresser of his vineyard, Behold, these three years I come seeking fruit on this fig tree, and find none: cut it down; why cumbereth it the ground? And he answering said unto him, Lord, let it alone this year also, till I shall dig about it, and dung it: and if it bear fruit, well; and if not, then after that thou shalt cut it down.

". . . Then said one unto Him, Lord, are there

few that be saved? And He said unto them: Strive to enter in at the strait gate: for many, I say unto you, will seek to enter in, and shall not be able. When once the master of the house is risen up, and hath shut to the door, and ye begin to stand without, and to knock at the door, saying, Lord, Lord, open unto us; and he shall answer and say unto you, I know you not whence ye are: then shall ye begin to say, We have eaten and drunk in thy presence, and thou hast taught in our streets. But he shall say, I tell you, I know you not whence ye are. Depart from me, all ye workers of iniquity. There shall be weeping and gnashing of teeth, when ye shall see Abraham, and Isaac, and Jacob, and all the prophets, in the kingdom of God, and you yourselves thrust out" (Luke 13:1-9, 23-28).

This passage from Luke's Gospel is one of *the greatest sermons* ever preached by the Lord Jesus Christ in His earthly ministry. There is a strange sequence of thought in these verses. The three pictures brought together in this one chapter present a complete evangelical message which is drastically needed today. Of course any one of the three pictures is a complete message within itself, but each of them contributes to the others, and *together* they point out the greatest need of mankind today.

No one could deny that Jesus was the greatest Preacher who ever preached. He knew *what* to say, He knew *how much* to say, and *everything He said was TRUTH because HE is truth!* (John 14:6).   He knew the illustrations which would drive home the tremendous truths of spiritual need and application.

The introduction to His sermon as given in the Scripture quoted in our text is contained in the first five verses. Jesus compared His listeners to "the Galilaeans whose blood Pilate had mingled with their sacrifices," and with "those eighteen upon whom the tower in Siloam fell, and slew them."   These references, while not elaborated upon in His sermon, were undoubtedly familiar to His listeners, and the comparison was unmistakable as He asked, "Suppose ye that these . . . were sinners above all Galilaeans . . . above all men that dwelt in Jerusalem?"   And then He drove home the truth of the comparison:

"Nay! but except YE repent, YE shall all likewise perish! . . . Nay, but except YE REPENT, ye shall all LIKEWISE perish!"

To fully appreciate these words, we must consider the fact that Jesus was not speaking to drunkards, gamblers, thieves, and other notable sinners. He was speaking to the *religious leaders* of His day—the men who boasted of being "Abraham's seed" and custodians of the oracles of God.   The Pharisees were proud, self-righteous religionists, and Jesus was plainly telling them that they must repent of their sins—or spend eternity in hell!

Perhaps some of these very same people had pointed out that the Galilaeans were slain and the eighteen men killed by the fall of the tower of Siloam because they were sinners, and God had meted out judgment to them because of their wickedness. But Jesus, in no uncertain terms, put the religionists under the same condemnation: *"Except YE repent, YE shall likewise perish!"*

In other words, Jesus said to them, "You religionists are no better off than those people! You *must* repent of your sins. Your boasting of being Abraham's seed, members of God's elect nation, will not help you in eternity. You must repent of your sins—or you will perish as did the Galilaeans and the men at Siloam."

Mark it and mark it well, dear reader: If you do not know Christ in the forgiveness of your sins, *YOU, too, must repent*—or perish. There is no salvation apart from true repentance—godly sorrow for sin, and turning face-about. And when a person turns to Jesus in true Bible repentance, he automatically turns his back on sin and the devil.

If the Lord Jesus Christ should step into some of our modern pulpits next Sunday morning, His message would still be *"Except you REPENT, you PERISH!"* Such preaching is not popular today. The elite, the sophisticated, the educated religionists detour around what they call the "old-fashioned, butcher-house religion." They have substituted a streamlined, polished, "easy" form which says, "Come forward and give me your hand . . . make a decision . . . join the church of your choice and then attend its services." It is true that there are thousands of God's men who are preaching the pure Gospel; but there are other thousands who are selling the Lord down the river for the sake of popularity, promotions, favor with the denominational leaders, and the praise of men. Jesus Christ is the same—yesterday, today, forever (Heb. 13:8), and God's Word still stresses the absolute necessity of repentance if sinners are to be saved.

After driving home the divine necessity for repentance, Jesus went on to declare that *opportunities do not last forever.* He said, "A certain man had *a fig tree* planted in his *vineyard;* and he came and sought fruit thereon, and found none. Then said he unto the dresser of his vineyard, *Behold, these three years I come seeking fruit on this fig tree, and find none. Cut it down! Why cumbereth it the ground?* And he answering said unto him, Lord, let it alone this year also, till I shall dig about it, and dung it: and if it bear fruit, well: and *if not, then after that THOU shalt cut it down"* (Luke 13:6-9).

Now anyone knows that a fig tree in the middle of a grape vineyard is certainly out of place! Yet this man had allowed a fig tree to grow for three years in the midst of his vineyard. Why? There can be only one sensible answer: the man who owned the grape vineyard *loved FIGS.* But the sad note here is that the owner of the vineyard had visited the fig tree for three successive years and found no figs on it. So when he came the third year and the tree was still barren, he said to the keeper of the vineyard, "Three years I have sought fruit on this tree and have found none. *Cut it down!* Why cumbereth it the ground?"

The keeper of the vineyard begged for the tree to be spared for one more year, during which time he would cultivate and fertilize the ground around it and give it every encouragement and opportunity to bear fruit. And then, if it still bore no fruit, *the OWNER of the vineyard should cut it down.*

Now if we are to understand what Jesus was teaching in this parable, we must first understand what the *fig tree* represents in the Word of God. In Jeremiah 24:1-5 we read:

"The Lord shewed me, and, behold, two baskets of figs were set before the temple of the Lord, after that Nebuchadrezzar king of Babylon had carried away captive Jeconiah the son of Jehoiakim king of Judah, and the princes of Judah, with the carpenters and smiths, from Jerusalem, and had brought them to Babylon. One basket had very good figs, even like the figs that are first ripe: and the other basket had very naughty figs, which could not be eaten, they were so bad. Then said the Lord unto me, What seest thou, Jeremiah? And I said, Figs; the good figs, very good; and the evil, very evil, that cannot be eaten, they are so evil.

"Again the Word of the Lord came unto me, saying, Thus saith the Lord, the God of Israel: Like these good figs, so will I acknowledge them that are carried away captive of Judah, whom I have sent out of this place into the land of the Chaldeans for their good."

The fig tree in the Bible represents the nation Israel, and when Jesus gave the parable of the fig tree in the midst of a vineyard He was *speaking* to people of that nation. If you will read the remaining verses in Jeremiah chapter 24 you will see that the figs mentioned in that chapter represent Israel in Palestine, in their own land. The *bad figs* are a symbol of Judah, the tribe from which the Jews came.

With this in mind, our parable begins to open up—a fig tree in the midst of a vineyard. The *earth* is God's great vineyard, and the twelve tribes of Israel were His chosen people. It is a settled fact that when Jesus came the first time He came to the lost sheep of the house of Israel (Matt. 15:24-28), and for three years He offered the kingdom to them. He sought them, wrought miracles among them, healed the sick, raised the dead, fed the hungry, and offered them the bread of life. During three years of His earthly ministry He walked the shores of Galilee and the dusty roads of Judaea, preaching and proclaiming the truth of His deity—the only begotten Son of Jehovah God, Israel's promised Messiah.

For example, He declared, "The Son of man is come to seek and to save that which was lost" (Luke 19:10).

He invited, "Come unto me, all ye that labour and are heavy laden, and I will give you rest" (Matt. 11:28).

"If any man thirst, let him come unto me, and drink. He that believeth on me, as the Scripture hath said, out of his belly shall flow rivers of living water" (John 7:37, 38).

"I am the resurrection and the life: he that believeth in me, though he were dead, yet shall he live: and whosoever liveth and believeth in me shall never die" (John 11:25, 26).

But the people of Israel shouted, "Away with Him! We will not have this Man to reign over us. Crucify Him—give us Barabbas!"

It was near the end of the third year of His public ministry that Jesus gave the parable of the barren fig tree. For three years He sought fruit in the nation of Israel, and the keeper of the vineyard, asking another year, sets forth the truth that Jesus gave them almost another year after the parable was given.

When they put Him to death they thought they had cut Him off; but Romans chapter 11 plainly declares that when the Jews crucified Jesus they cut *themselves* off from the natural olive tree, and the *wild* olive branch (the Gentiles) was grafted in. Of course a few individual Jews are being saved during this Dispensation of Grace; but Israel as a nation is spiritually blind and will remain so until Jesus returns to earth. When the King comes in great glory, when He stands on the Mount of Olives and Israel sees the scars in His hands and feet (Zech. 13:6; 14:4) they will recognize and own Him as Messiah and a nation will be saved in a day (Isa. 66:8; Rom. 11:26).

Writing to the Christians at Rome, the Apostle Paul (himself a Jew) explains the present position of the Jewish nation in this Dispensation of Grace:

"I say then, Hath God cast away His people? God forbid! For I also am an Israelite, of the seed of Abraham, of the tribe of Benjamin. God HATH NOT cast away His people which He foreknew. Wot ye not what the Scripture saith of Elias? how he maketh intercession to God against Israel, saying, Lord, they have killed thy prophets, and digged down thine altars; and I am left alone, and they seek my life. But what saith the answer of God unto him? I have reserved to myself seven thousand men, who have not bowed the knee to the image of Baal. Even so then *at this present time also there is a remnant according to THE ELECTION OF GRACE.* . . .

"What then? Israel hath not obtained that which he seeketh for; but the election hath obtained it, *and the rest were blinded* (according

101

as it is written, God hath given them the spirit of slumber, eyes that they should not see, and ears that they should not hear;) *unto this day. . . .*

"I say then, Have they stumbled that they should fall? God forbid: but rather through their fall salvation is come unto the Gentiles, for to provoke them to jealousy. Now if the fall of them be the riches of the world, and the diminishing of them the riches of the Gentiles; how much more their fulness? . . . For if the casting away of them be the reconciling of the world, what shall the receiving of them be, but life from the dead? For if the firstfruit be holy, the lump is also holy: and if the root be holy, so are the branches. . . .

"For if thou wert cut out of the olive tree which is wild by nature, and wert graffed contrary to nature into a good olive tree: how much more shall these, which be the natural branches, be graffed into their own olive tree? For I would not, brethren, that ye should be ignorant of this mystery, lest ye should be wise in your own conceits; that *blindness in part is happened to Israel, until the fulness of the Gentiles be come in. And so ALL ISRAEL shall be saved:* as it is written, There shall come out of Sion the Deliverer, and shall turn away ungodliness from Jacob: for this is my covenant unto them, when I shall take away their sins.

"As concerning the Gospel, they are enemies for your sakes: but as touching the election, they are beloved for the fathers' sakes. *For the gifts and calling of God are WITHOUT REPENTANCE.* For as ye in times past have not believed God, yet have now obtained mercy through their unbelief: even so have these also now not believed, that through your mercy they also may obtain mercy. For God hath concluded them all in unbelief, that He might have mercy upon all" (Rom. 11:1-32 in part).

It was through unbelief that Israel became blinded in part. They rejected their Messiah through the three years of His earthly ministry, and as the barren fig tree was to be cut down if it bore no fruit, the parable showed unfruitful and rebellious Israel that God's patience with them would come to an end if they persisted in going their own way.

However, Jesus did not pronounce a benediction after the parable of the fig tree, but went even a step further and used a second outstanding and familiar illustration in an effort to bear home to their hearts the solemn fact that *opportunities pass swiftly away:*

"When once the master of the house is risen up, and hath shut to the door, and ye begin to stand without, and to knock at the door, saying, Lord, Lord, open unto us; and he shall answer and say unto you, I know you not . . . depart from me, all ye workers of iniquity" (Luke 13:25, 27).

In the second passage of our Scripture text,

Jesus was asked, "Lord, are there few that be saved?" He replied with the illustration given in verse 25. We can better understand His meaning if we consider the cities of that day. Every city had a great wall around it, with gates in the wall. At sundown, the gates were closed and locked, not to be opened again until morning. The people to whom Jesus was speaking knew full well the tragedy of being left outside the gates of a city at night. There were guards who patroled the walls, and at evening as the guards prepared to close the great iron gates, people came hurrying to get inside. Camel drivers rushed their animals, people on foot came in great haste, some running, to get inside the walls before the gates clanged shut.

But suppose two old friends met and stopped to greet each other. They were but a short distance from the gate, perhaps they did not realize the lateness of the hour. But while they talked, the sound of a bugle pierced the air and they heard the screech of great hinges as the gate swung shut. They rushed up to the gate and cried for entrance. They pounded frantically on the gate and called out to the guards to let them in. But the "master of the house" had ordered the gates of the city to be closed, and they would not be opened to admit those who had not entered before the appointed time when the city was locked away for the night.

The master of the house called out to those outside, "I do not know you, I do not know from whence you are." Then the travelers explained, "We ate and drank in your presence. You taught in our streets. Surely you remember us!" But the master of the house replied, "I tell you, I know not whence ye are. Depart from me, all ye workers of iniquity!" And the next verse tells us, "There shall be weeping and gnashing of teeth." Those left outside the city gates would be greatly disturbed because they know that robbers and highwaymen will take advantage of the darkness to prey upon travelers along the road and those outside the protection of the city walls.

"Strive to enter in at the strait gate: for many, I say unto you, will seek to enter in, *and shall not be able*" (Luke 13:24). By this statement did Jesus mean that many would seek to be saved, but *could not* be saved? Did He mean that many would seek salvation *but could not find it?* No indeed. That is not the meaning of this verse. Verse 25 clears up any vague ideas concerning the meaning here. Jesus said, "When once the master of the house is risen up, and hath *shut to the door . . . ,*" making it very clear that He was teaching that *opportunities do not last forever* and can *quickly pass away.* Just as travelers must obey the laws of the road and the laws of the city if they hope for the protection of the guards and the city walls, so must we, if we hope to go to

105

heaven, obey God's Word—*HIS way, not OUR way.*

God is a God of law and order. We are not under the Law of Moses, but under the laws of God. The Bible commands, "Ye must be born again," and those who *refuse* to be born again in this life can beat on heaven's door all they please but they will not get in! Jesus declared, *"I am the DOOR"* (John 10:9). Webster's dictionary defines a door as "a moveable structure for opening or closing a doorway." In other words, the hole in the wall is the *doorway,* and the structure that opens or closes the doorway is the *door.* Jesus is the Door to heaven—He is the One through whom you must *enter* heaven, and there is *only ONE Door, one WAY to that blessed abode.* If you put off receiving Jesus in this life, on the other side of the grave He will see to it that you do not enter heaven to spend eternity with Him.

The people in the parable Jesus gave either wasted their time along the road, started too late, or traveled too slowly, and their opportunity passed, *wasted.* The gate was shut, and in spite of the fact that they declared acquaintance with the master of the house, they did not get inside. By this parable He was telling the Jews very plainly that He had taught in the streets of Jerusalem, they had been present when He fed the five thousand, they had eaten of the loaves and the fishes. He had performed such miracles in their presence as only God could perform. Therefore, since they *refused to acknowledge Him*, in the life to come He will say to them, "I know you not!"

In Matthew 10:32, 33 Jesus plainly declared, "Whosoever therefore shall confess me before men, him will I confess also before my Father which is in heaven. But whosoever shall *deny* me before men, him will I also deny before my Father which is in heaven." *Today* is the day of salvation, *now* is the accepted time (II Cor. 6:2).

Unsaved friend, keep this in mind: If you shake your head in God's face now and refuse His salvation, be not surprised when He shakes His head in *your* face and declares at the gates of heaven, "I know you not!" Jesus pointed out to the Jews that they were *right then* having opportunity to be saved, opportunity to accept Him as Messiah and Saviour, but the opportunity would not last forever. They did not accept Him then, they continued to rebel against Him, and when they demanded His death they sealed their destiny and signed their own death warrant. In 70 A. D. Titus the Roman butchered five million Jews in Jerusalem and surrounding areas, and leveled that city to the ground with not one stone left upon another! The Jews learned the hard way that opportunities do not last forever, they can swiftly pass away. Theirs did—*and YOURS may!*

Another important point in the sermon Jesus preached that day is the fact that *opportunities rejected seldom return.* As He wept over His beloved city of Jerusalem, He said, "O Jerusalem, Jerusalem, which killest the prophets, and stonest them that are sent unto thee; how often would I have gathered thy children together, as a hen doth gather her brood under her wings—*and ye would not! Behold, your house is left unto you desolate:* and verily I say unto you, Ye shall not see me, until the time come when ye shall say, Blessed is He that cometh in the name of the Lord" (Luke 13:34, 35).

Please notice Jesus did not say, "Your house is *going to be* left unto you desolate." He said, "Your house *IS left* unto you desolate." That is, "You have rejected your last opportunity to accept salvation. Therefore your house is left desolate and will be destroyed." Jesus foresaw the horrors that would soon befall Jerusalem, the terrible miseries that would soon come upon the inhabitants of that city.

He foresaw the destruction of the temple, and said to His disciples, "See ye not all these things? Verily I say unto you, There shall not be left here one stone upon another, that shall not be thrown down" (Matt. 24:2).

He foresaw the inhuman suffering which would befall the mothers among His people. At the crucifixion, as a great company of women bewailed and lamented Him, He turned to them and said, "Daughters of Jerusalem, weep not for me, but weep for yourselves, and for your children. For, behold, the days are coming, in the which they shall say, Blessed are the barren, and the wombs that never bare, and the paps which never gave suck" (Luke 23:27-29).

The Prophet Jeremiah wrote, "Thus saith the Lord: A voice was heard in Ramah, lamentation, and bitter weeping; Rahel weeping for her children refused to be comforted for her children, because they were not" (Jer. 31:15).

Knowing what destruction and horror was to fall upon the Holy City, Jerusalem, in the near future, Jesus wept over the city—so near unto salvation, yet rejecting His last invitation! Never again would that generation be visited by the Son of God. Never again would they hear His tender voice—"Come unto me. . . . I will in no wise cast you out. . . . If the Son shall make you free, you shall be free indeed!"

As God looks down on this great land of America today and sees the drunkenness, sin, lust, and shame, I wonder if His great heart is not grieved as the heart of Jesus was grieved when He wept over Jerusalem? I wonder if God does not say, "O, America! America! How I would love to gather you unto myself—*and ye will not*"? America has had so many golden opportunities and has turned them down. She has turned God's Holy Day into a holiday. She worships her own gods—gods of pleasure, sports, fortune and fame. God would love to save America, and if He could send just one short chapter to this country today I wonder what it would be? I wonder if, as a nation, we are weighed in God's balances and found wanting?

And how can Christ's sermon be applied to our own lives? First of all, we should, as He told the Jews, "strive to enter in at the strait gate." In the words of Peter, "Give diligence to make your calling and election sure: for if ye do these things, ye shall never fall" (II Pet. 1:10). Opportunities can pass so swiftly! Today is the day, now is the time, ten minutes from now the door to heaven may be shut for you if you are not saved. God's Word warns, "Boast not thyself of to morrow; for thou knowest not what a day may bring forth" (Prov. 27:1).

In Proverbs 1:24-29 God declares, "Because I have called, and ye refused; I have stretched out my hand, and no man regarded; but ye have set at nought all my counsel, and would none of my reproof: I also will laugh at your calamity; I will mock when your fear cometh; when your fear cometh as desolation, and your destruction cometh as a whirlwind; when distress and anguish cometh upon you. Then shall they call upon me, but I will not answer. They shall seek me early, but they shall not find me: for that they hated knowledge, and did not choose the fear of the Lord!"

Beloved, if in your heart you feel a desire to be saved, you have not crossed God's deadline. You still have the opportunity, the invitation to be saved. Do not longer reject Jesus, lest this be your *last* opportunity and when your fear cometh, God may laugh at your calamity.

As Jesus pointed out to the Jews, opportunities do not last forever, and if you reject this opportunity to be saved, one of these days you will remember—in hell—the many golden opportunities you had to be saved in this life. You will remember reading this sermon. You will remember every sermon you ever heard preached and every invitation hymn you ever heard sung. You will remember every altar call you turned down. When the rich man in hell begged for a drop of water to cool his parching tongue, father Abraham replied, *"Son, REMEMBER . . . in thy lifetime . . ."* (Luke 16:25). A person who drops into the pits of the damned carries with him *all five senses*. There will be memories in hell, and I personally believe the hell of memory will be much more tormenting than the flames of hell's fire!

So ask yourself sincerely, "Will this be my last opportunity to be saved?" It could be! You are breathing God's air, enjoying the life God gave you, and He can take that life from you, even before this day is over! Jesus declared, "Except a man be *born again,* he cannot see the kingdom of God" (John 3:3). Church membership

111

will not save you, baptism will not save you, good works will not save you. *You MUST be born again,* and there is *only one way* to be born again *—GOD'S way.* God furnishes the power for the new birth when you receive the Lord Jesus into your heart by faith:

"As many as received Him, to them gave He power to become the sons of God, even to them that believe on His name: which were born, not of blood, nor of the will of the flesh, nor of the will of man, but of God" (John 1:12, 13).

Ephesians 2:8, 9 tells us, *"By GRACE are ye saved through faith,* and that not of yourselves: it is the gift of God: not of works, lest any man should boast."

Romans 10:9, 10 explains, "If thou shalt confess with thy mouth the Lord Jesus, and shalt believe in thine heart that God hath raised Him from the dead, thou shalt be saved. For with the heart man believeth unto righteousness; and with the mouth confession is made unto salvation."

Beloved, if you do not know you are saved just as surely as you know the color of your skin, I beg you to believe these Scriptures, do what they tell you to do, and God will "born" you into His family. If you are not saved, give your heart to Jesus now; *and if you ARE saved,* bow your head and thank God that you are His child!

The Righteous vs. the Wicked

The Righteous vs. the Wicked

"Fret not thyself because of evildoers, neither be thou envious against the workers of iniquity. For they shall soon be cut down like the grass, and wither as the green herb. Trust in the Lord, and do good; so shalt thou dwell in the land, and verily thou shalt be fed.

"Delight thyself also in the Lord; and He shall give thee the desires of thine heart. Commit thy way unto the Lord; trust also in Him; and He shall bring it to pass. And He shall bring forth thy righteousness as the light, and thy judgment as the noonday.

"Rest in the Lord, and wait patiently for Him: fret not thyself because of him who prospereth in his way, because of the man who bringeth wicked devices to pass. Cease from anger, and forsake wrath: fret not thyself in any wise to do evil. For evildoers shall be cut off: but those that wait upon the Lord, they shall inherit the earth.

"For yet a little while, and the wicked shall not be: yea, thou shalt diligently consider his place, and it shall not be. But the meek shall inherit the earth; and shall delight themselves in the abundance of peace. The wicked plotteth against the just, and gnasheth upon him with his teeth. The Lord shall laugh at him: for He seeth that his day is coming. The wicked have drawn out the sword, and have bent their bow, to cast down the poor and needy, and to slay such as be of upright conversation. Their sword shall enter into their own heart, and their bows shall be broken.

"A little that a righteous man hath is better than the riches of many wicked. For the arms of the wicked shall be broken: but the Lord upholdeth the righteous. The Lord knoweth the days of the upright: and their inheritance shall be for ever. They shall not be ashamed in the evil time: and in the days of famine they shall be satisfied.

"But the wicked shall perish, and the enemies of the Lord shall be as the fat of lambs: they shall consume; into smoke shall they consume away. The wicked borroweth, and payeth not again: but the righteous sheweth mercy, and giveth. For such as be blessed of him shall inherit the earth; and they that be cursed of him shall be cut off.

"The steps of a good man are ordered by the Lord: and he delighteth in His way. Though he fall, he shall not be utterly cast down: for the Lord upholdeth him with His hand. I have been young, and now am old; yet have I not seen the righteous forsaken, nor his seed begging bread.

He is ever merciful, and lendeth; and his seed is blessed.

"Depart from evil, and do good; and dwell for evermore. For the Lord loveth judgment, and forsaketh not His saints. They are preserved for ever: but the seed of the wicked shall be cut off. The righteous shall inherit the land, and dwell therein for ever. The mouth of the righteous speaketh wisdom, and his tongue talketh of judgment. The law of his God is in his heart; none of his steps shall slide.

"The wicked watcheth the righteous, and seeketh to slay him. The Lord will not leave him in his hand, nor condemn him when he is judged. Wait on the Lord, and keep His way, and He shall exalt thee to inherit the land: when the wicked are cut off, thou shalt see it. I have seen the wicked in great power, and spreading himself like a green bay tree. Yet he passed away, and, lo, he was not: yea, I sought him, but he could not be found.

"Mark the perfect man, and behold the upright: for the end of that man is peace. But the transgressors shall be destroyed together: the end of the wicked shall be cut off. But the salvation of the righteous is of the Lord: He is their strength in the time of trouble. And the Lord shall help them, and deliver them: He shall deliver them from the wicked, and save them, because they trust in Him" (Psalm 37:1-40).

Behold the Man!

God knows only two classes of people that dwell on the earth (the righteous and the unrighteous) and in this Psalm the Holy Spirit makes clear distinction between the two. Inspired of God, the Psalmist makes three unmistakable comparisons between the godly and the ungodly:

1. He gives the names of the wicked and the names of the righteous.

2. He shows the attitude of the wicked toward the righteous, and the attitude of the righteous toward the wicked.

3. He compares the final state of the wicked and the final state of the righteous.

We will study each of these comparisons in turn, using only the Word of God as our textbook.

Names of the Wicked

In the Psalm just quoted we find six different names applied to the wicked:

1. "Evildoers" (vv. 1, 9).
2. "Workers of iniquity" (v. 1).
3. "The wicked" (vv. 10, 12, 14, 16, 17, 20, 21, 28, 32, 34, 35, 38, 40).
4. "Enemies of the Lord" (v. 20).
5. "They that be cursed" (v. 22).
6. "Transgressors" (v. 38).

These names are descriptive of the *character* of the wicked. They represent the actual *condition* of those who know not God. *"God is LIGHT, and in Him is no darkness at all"* (I John 1:5), but in the wicked He sees total darkness. There is not one iota of goodness (as *God* measures goodness) in the unbeliever, and he might well be described in the words of Isaiah: ". . . the whole head is sick, and the whole heart faint. From the sole of the foot even unto the head there is no soundness in it; but wounds, and bruises, and putrifying sores . . ." (Isa. 1:5, 6).

In his letter to the Christians in Rome, the Apostle Paul describes unbelievers, both Jew and Gentile, as being "under sin," and declares, "As it is written, *There is NONE righteous, no, not ONE!* There is none that understandeth, there is none that seeketh after God. They are all gone out of the way, they are together become unprofitable; there is none that doeth good, no, not one. Their throat is an open sepulchre; with their tongues they have used deceit; the poison of asps is under their lips: whose mouth is full of cursing and bitterness. Their feet are swift to shed blood: destruction and misery are in their ways: and the way of peace have they not known. There is no fear of God before their eyes. Now we know that what things soever the law saith, it saith to them who are under the law, *that every mouth may be stopped, and ALL THE WORLD may become guilty before God"* (Rom. 3:10-19).

What a horrible, sickening picture of unregenerate man! and *Isaiah* emphatically declares that even "our *righteousnesses* (that is, the very best

we can do) are as *filthy rags"* in the sight of God
(Isa. 64:6).

In Psalm 37 David is not discussing the wicked
in relationship *to one another,* nor is he discussing
the wicked in their *human "goodness."* He is
describing the wicked in their relationship to a
holy God and to God's people. In II Kings 5:1 we
read that Naaman was "a great man . . . honour-
able . . . a mighty man in valour" — and then we
read these sad words: *"but he was a LEPER."*
In the Word of God, leprosy is a type of sin; and
just as leprosy prevented Naaman's being wholly
clean, so the unbeliever can be nothing but un-
cleanness in the sight of God, no matter how
humanly "good" he may be. The sinner *before
God* is totally depraved, there is not one good
thing about him. He is an evildoer, a worker of
iniquity, a transgressor against a holy God. He
is God's enemy and is therefore under the curse
of God.

There is much ignorance among church people
concerning unbelievers. They are referred to as
"good" men or "good" women, they are described
as being honest, upright, clean, respectable. This
may all be true insofar as man sees and insofar
as it is possible for man to judge; but when God
looks down on mankind He sees only two classes
of people — the *holy* and the *unholy,* sons of *God,*
and sons of *the devil.* Jesus Himself made it very
clear that there is no neutrality before God. We

are for Him, or we are against Him. Jesus said, "He that is not *with* me is *against* me; and he that *gathereth* not with me *scattereth abroad*" (Matt. 12:30).

Names of the Righteous

The Psalm in our text also records six names applied to the righteous:
1. "The meek" (v. 11).
2. "The just" (v. 12).
3. "The upright" (vv. 18, 37).
4. The "good man" (v. 23).
5. God's "saints" (v. 28).
6. "The righteous" (vv. 16, 17, 21, 25, 29, 30, 32, 39).

These names describe the character of the believer *as God sees him—IN CHRIST;* and one *becomes* righteous *only* in Christ (Col. 1:27, 28).

You will notice in the names given to the wicked and to the righteous, the Holy Spirit says not one *good thing* about the wicked, nor does He ascribe one *evil thing* to the righteous. This does not mean that the unbeliever does not possess human goodness, nor does it mean that the righteous have no carnality about them. It simply means that the enemies of God are *total* enemies. There is not one good thing about them, spiritually speaking. They are evil, they are workers of iniquity, they are transgressors against God. They can be nothing else as long as they remain in unbelief. The Apostle Paul reminds us that it was while we were yet *sinners* that Christ died for us, that we might be justified by His blood and reconciled to God (Rom. 5:8-10), and until the sinner comes under the blood of Jesus through faith in His finished work, *the wrath of God abides on him.*

By contrast, *believers* are covered by the cleansing blood of the Lamb of God, *righteousness* has been imputed to them, and in the sight of God they are therefore *just as though they had never sinned.* When God looks upon the believer He sees the righteousness, holiness, and purity of His only begotten Son. Thus the believer is "accepted in the Beloved" (Eph. 1:6), his sins are covered by the blood, and God remembers them against him no more (Heb. 10:17).

As I prepare this sermon for the press, I am fifty-four years old *in the flesh;* but insofar as God is concerned He has no record concerning me up to the day I was born again thirty-six years ago. I am thirty-six years old in the Lord, and the years of my life up to the time I was born again have been completely erased from God's record, and forgotten. He sees me *only IN CHRIST, righteous and complete.* Hallelujah!

The born again believer stands in the presence of God *justified.* God's Word promises, "Though your sins be as scarlet, they shall be *as white as snow;* though they be red like crimson, *they shall be as wool"* (Isa. 1:18). Jesus bore our sins in His own body on the cross, and when we are covered by His precious blood we are made the righteousness of God in Him:

"For what saith the Scripture? Abraham believed God, and it was counted unto him for righteousness. . . . To him that worketh not, but believeth on Him that justifieth the ungodly, his faith is counted for righteousness. Even as David also describeth the blessedness of the man, unto whom God imputeth righteousness without works, saying, Blessed are they whose iniquities are forgiven, and whose sins are covered" (Rom. 4:3-7 in part).

God made Jesus to be sin for us, that we might be made the righteousness of God in Him (II Cor. 5:21), and "there is therefore now *NO condemnation* to them which are *IN CHRIST JESUS* . . . for the law of the Spirit of life in Christ Jesus hath made (us) free from the law of sin and death. For what the law could not do, in that it was weak through the flesh, God sending His own Son in the likeness of sinful flesh, and for sin, condemned sin in the flesh: that the righteousness of the law might be fulfilled in us, who walk not after the flesh, but after the Spirit" (Rom. 8:1-4).

It will be a happy day in the lives of many believers when they recognize the fact that they are saved with a perfect salvation prepared and provided by a perfect God. When a person is justified through the blood of Jesus, that person is righteous, holy, just, pure, and spotless in the sight of God. On the other hand, the person *not justified* is in total darkness—hopeless, helpless, strengthless, an enemy to God and bound for hell! Regardless of how much "good" one is doing, how many good works he may accomplish or how uprightly moral he may be in his life, all of man's goodness adds up to nothing but filthy rags in the sight of God!

The Attitude of the Wicked Toward the Righteous

"The wicked plotteth against the just, and gnasheth upon him with his teeth. . . . The wicked have drawn out the sword, and have bent their bow, to cast down the poor and needy, and to slay such as be of upright conversation. . . . The wicked watcheth the righteous, and seeketh to slay him" (Psalm 37:12, 14, 32).

An example of verse 12 is seen in the treatment Stephen received at the hands of the wicked. Stephen is described as being "full of faith and power," and the members of the synagogue who spoke against him and disputed with him "were not able to resist the wisdom and the Spirit by which he spake" (Acts 6:8, 10). In his sermon before the council, Stephen described the enemies of the Gospel so minutely, and they became so angry with him, that they *"gnashed on him with their teeth* . . . and ran upon him with one accord, and cast him out of the city and stoned him" (Acts 7:54-58)—in fact, they stoned him to death. He is recorded as having been the first martyr of the New Testament Church.

The wicked have not changed their minds about the saints of God until this very day in which we live. It is true that we do not hear of people being "gnashed upon" with the teeth, but I feel persuaded in my own heart that if we who preach the Gospel today were as bold as Stephen was, and if we preached with the uncompromising clarity and power with which he preached, we would be stoned and perhaps "gnashed on" by the wicked of this day. But this is the age of compromise, and there are very few men who stand as steadfastly as Stephen did in declaring the whole counsel of God and rebuking the wicked for their wickedness!

Notice David describes the wicked as murderers. They "have drawn out *the sword*," they watch the righteous and seek to *slay* him (vv. 14, 32). They may not literally shed blood in every case, but those who are guilty of hatred are murderers nevertheless—and you can rest assured that the ungodly hate the righteous just as much today as they did in the days of Stephen, Paul, and other giants of the faith in the early days of Christianity.

Jesus said to His disciples, ". . . If they have called the Master of the house Beelzebub, how

much more shall they call them of His household?"
(Matt. 10:25). The enemies of Jesus called Him
every ugly name they could think of. In John 9:24
they declared, "We know that this Man is a sinner!" They accused Him of being an illegitimate,
born of fornication (John 8:41). They said He was
possessed of a devil (John 8:48, 52), "and many of
them said, He hath a devil, and is mad . . ." (John
10:20). They accused Him of casting out demons
by the power of Beelzebub, prince of demons (Matt.
12:24). They hated Him and plotted against Him
until finally they saw Him nailed to a Roman
cross—and even then they mocked Him as He died
to save even those who had demanded His death!

In John 15:18, 19 Jesus warned His disciples,
"If the world hate you, ye know that it hated
me before it hated *you*. If ye were *of* the world,
the world would love his own: but *because ye
are not of the world*, but I have chosen you *out*
of the world, therefore the world hateth you."

This has been true down through the ages.
The wicked have hated the righteous. The devil
is the god of this world, the prince of the power
of the air (II Cor. 4:4; Eph. 2:2), and he hates the
children of God as much as he hated the only
begotten *Son of God*. John the Beloved declares,
"We know that *we are of God*, and the whole
world lieth *in wickedness*"—or, in the lap of the
wicked one (I John 5:19). So we see that the attitude
of the world toward Christians has not changed

since the days when Jesus walked on earth.

HOWEVER — after warning His disciples that they would have tribulation as they lived for Him in this life, He *assured* them of *victory:* ". . . be of good cheer; *I have OVERCOME the world"* (John 16:33). Thus, regardless of temptation, trials, persecution and tribulation, *"we are MORE than conquerors* through Him that loved us. For . . . neither death, nor life, nor angels, nor principalities, nor powers, nor things present, nor things to come, nor height, nor depth, nor any other creature, shall be able to separate us from the love of God, which is in Christ Jesus our Lord!" (Rom. 8:37-39).

There can be no more love in the heart of an ungodly man toward the children of God than there is love in the heart of an ungodly man toward God Himself. All who surrender fully to Christ will meet with reproach and opposition — *"Yea, and ALL that will live godly in Christ Jesus SHALL suffer persecution!"* (II Tim. 3:12).

Hear the words of the Apostle Peter concerning the attitude of the wicked toward the righteous:

"Beloved, think it not strange concerning the fiery trial which is to try you, as though some strange thing happened unto you: *but REJOICE, inasmuch as ye are partakers of Christ's sufferings;* that, when His glory shall be revealed, ye may be glad also with exceeding joy. If ye be reproached for the name of Christ, happy are ye; for the Spirit of glory and of God resteth upon you: on their part He is evil spoken of, but on your part He is glorified.

"But let none of you suffer as a murderer, or as a thief, or as an evildoer, or as a busybody in other men's matters. Yet if any man suffer as a Christian, let him not be ashamed; but let him glorify God on this behalf. For the time is come that judgment must begin at the house of God: and if it first begin at us, what shall the end be of them that obey not the Gospel of God? And if the righteous scarcely be saved, where shall the ungodly and the sinner appear? Wherefore let them that suffer *ACCORDING TO THE WILL OF GOD* commit the keeping of their souls to Him in well doing, as unto a faithful Creator" (I Pet. 4:12-19).

Yes, "think it not strange" that believers are despised and persecuted by the wicked. When Jesus was born in Bethlehem, there was no room for Him in the inn (Luke 2:7). There was no room for Him in the temple when He drove out the money-changers and overthrew the money tables (John 2:13-16). There was no room for Him in the synagogue in His home town of Nazareth, and "they in the synagogue . . . rose up, and thrust Him out of the city, and led Him unto the brow of the hill whereon their city was built, that they might cast Him down headlong" (Luke 4:28, 29). There was no room for Him on the earth—"He was in the world, and the world was made by Him, and the world knew Him not. He came unto His own, and His own received Him not" (John 1:10, 11). The people of His own nation cried out, "Away with Him! Away with Him! Crucify Him!" (John 19:15)—and they chose a convicted robber and murderer instead of the Lord of glory.

So we need not think it strange when the wicked persecute the righteous. But whatever comes our way, "we know that all things work together for good to them that love God, to them who are the called according to His purpose. . . . What shall we then say to these things? *If God be FOR us, who can be AGAINST us?*" (Rom. 8:28, 31).

The Attitude of the Righteous
Toward the Wicked

"Fret not thyself because of evildoers, neither be thou envious against the workers of iniquity. . . . Rest in the Lord, and wait patiently for Him: fret not thyself because of him who prospereth in his way, because of the man who bringeth wicked devices to pass. Cease from anger, and forsake wrath: fret not thyself in any wise to do evil" (Psalm 37:1, 7, 8).

David does not develop the subject of the attitude of believers toward unbelievers as it is developed in other parts of the Word of God, but three times in the first eight verses he commands, *"Fret not!"* Thus we see that the Christian should not worry or be anxious because of evildoers, nor be envious because the wicked "prospereth in his way." Under no circumstance is a believer to become so fretful, anxious, and disturbed as to do evil against those who perpetrate evil against God's people and despitefully use them.

We see first of all the teaching of Jesus on what the attitude of the righteous toward the wicked should be. In Matthew 5:44 He said, *"LOVE your enemies,* bless them that curse you, do good to them that hate you, and pray for them which despitefully use you, and persecute you."

In Luke 6:31-35 Jesus instructed, "As ye would that men should do to you, do ye also to them likewise. For if ye love them which love you, what thank have ye? for sinners also love those that love them. And if ye do good to them which do good to you, what thank have ye? for sinners also do even the same. And if ye lend to them of whom ye hope to receive, what thank have ye? for sinners also lend to sinners, to receive as much again. But love ye your enemies, and do good, and lend, hoping for nothing again; and your reward shall be great, and ye shall be the children of the Highest: for He is kind unto the unthankful and to the evil."

The Apostle Paul gave *further instruction* concerning the attitude of believers toward unbelievers. In Romans 12:17-21 he wrote: "Recompense to no man evil for evil. Provide things honest in the sight of all men. If it be possible, as much as lieth in you, live peaceably with all men. Dearly beloved, avenge not yourselves, but rather give place unto wrath: for it is written, *Vengeance is MINE; I will repay,* saith the Lord.

"Therefore if thine enemy hunger, feed him. If he thirst, give him drink: for in so doing thou shalt heap coals of fire on his head. Be not overcome of evil, but overcome evil with good."

God's Word makes it very clear that believers are not to retaliate, we are not to recompense evil for evil. We are to live peaceably with all men insofar as is humanly possible. God Himself will take vengeance on those who do evil against His saints. Therefore we are to do good in return for evil. It is impossible to overcome evil with *evil,* but it is not impossible to overcome evil with *good,* and the righteous are to behave righteously toward the ungodly.

We are instructed not to fret or be envious of *"him who prospereth in HIS WAY."* The wicked prosper, to be sure. Many *unrighteous* men make money and acquire fame and fortune, while many *righteous* men have but the bare necessities of life. But notice the wicked prospers *in "HIS way,"* and HIS way is not *GOD'S way.* The unsaved person cannot bring glory to God, and Proverbs 21:4 tells us that even "the *plowing* of the wicked is sin." In other words, *whatever the Christian does* should be done to the glory

131

of God (I Cor. 10:31), but the *very best* an *unbeliever* can do will add up to no more than filthy rags (Isa. 64:6).

The concern of the righteous should be the instruction Jesus gave in Matthew 6:33: "Seek ye FIRST the kingdom of God, and His righteousness; and all these things shall be added unto you." The wicked may prosper all around us, but if we put God first in our lives and in all that we do, all necessary things will be added for our good and His glory. Paul assured the Philippian believers, "My God shall supply all your need according to His riches in glory by Christ Jesus" (Phil. 4:19).

Some of God's dearest saints have been in wheelchairs or on beds of affliction for years, and many of them have never had more than the bare necessities of life; while ungodly men and women have prospered, enjoyed good health, and been able to afford all the good things of this life. But we must remember that all the joy and pleasure the wicked will ever know will come to them in this life, while the righteous will live eternally in the Pearly White City in the presence of God. The wicked have their reward in this life, and when they depart this life they will die eternally in the lake of fire. *"The wicked shall be turned into hell,* and all the nations that forget God" (Psalm 9:17).

The prophet Isaiah declares, "The wicked are

like the troubled sea, when it cannot rest, whose waters cast up mire and dirt. There is no peace, saith my God, to the wicked" (Isa. 57:20, 21). But Jesus *bequeathed* peace to the Christian—"Peace I leave with you, *MY peace* I give unto you: not as the world giveth, give I unto you. Let not your heart be troubled, neither let it be afraid" (John 14:27). Hebrews 4:9 tells us, "There remaineth therefore *a REST to the people of God."* Resting on God's Word, surely we have no cause to fret or be envious when the wicked prosper, or when they commit evil against us! How wonderful and blessed it is to realize our nothingness and God's all-sufficiency! We possess everything in Jesus.

The End of the Wicked

"They shall soon be *cut down like the grass,* and *wither as the green herb.* . . . Evildoers shall be *cut off.* . . . Yet a little while, and *the wicked shall not be.* . . . The Lord shall laugh at him. . . . Their sword shall enter into their own heart, and their bows shall be broken. . . . The wicked shall *perish* . . . they shall *consume;* into smoke shall they *consume away.* . . . The transgressors shall be *destroyed* together: *the end of the wicked shall be cut off."*

These exerpts, taken from our text of Psalm 37, plainly tell us what the end of the wicked will be! As we look around us today, the wicked seem

133

to be on the winning side. Those who practice evil seem to prosper and flourish, corruption is on every hand. Many of the ungodly live in fine homes, drive fine cars, wear fine clothes—but just as a picture cannot be rightly judged until the finished product is framed and hung on the wall, so we cannot judge the end of the wicked until it actually occurs. God has spoken; and regardless of how the present state of affairs may look, the end will be total destruction, eternal death and damnation for those who know not God!

The Psalmist further says of the wicked, ". . . God is angry with the wicked every day. . . . His mischief shall return upon his own head, and his violent dealing shall come down upon his own pate" (Psalm 7:11b, 16). Romans 6:23 warns, *"The wages of sin is DEATH,"* and James 1:15 tells us that *sin, when it is finished, "bringeth forth DEATH."* This speaks of *eternal* death, death in the lake of fire that burns with brimstone forever. Eternal misery awaits the wicked in the regions of the damned. The path of the wicked is the path to destruction. It may be smooth, it may be a broad way, it may seem to be filled with joy; but it will climax in darkness, despair, misery, and eternal torment in hell. Oh, yes—regardless of what man may think or say about hell, *there IS such a place,* and the Word of God plainly tells us that it was prepared for the devil and his angels, and for all who choose to serve the devil in this life (Matt. 25:41).

David, a man after God's own heart, encountered discouragement and uncertainty when he saw how the wicked prospered. But God revealed to him *the ultimate END of the wicked,* and then he rejoiced that he had put his trust in the Lord. In Psalm 73 he wrote:

". . . As for me, my feet were almost gone; my steps had well nigh slipped. For I was envious at the foolish, when I saw the prosperity of the wicked. . . . They are not in trouble as other men; neither are they plagued like other men. Therefore pride compasseth them about as a chain; violence covereth them as a garment. Their eyes stand out with fatness: they have more than heart could wish. They are corrupt, and speak wickedly concerning oppression: they speak loftily. They set their mouth against the heavens, and their tongue walketh through the earth. . . . And they say, How doth God know? and is there knowledge in the most High?

"Behold, these are the ungodly, who prosper in the world. They increase in riches. Verily I have cleansed my heart in vain, and washed my hands in innocency. For all the day long have I been plagued, and chastened every morning. . . . When I thought to know this, it was too painful for me—*until I went into the sanctuary of GOD; then understood I their END.* Surely thou didst set them in slippery places: thou castedst them down into destruction. How are they brought into desolation, as in a moment! They are utterly consumed with terrors.

". . . Nevertheless I am continually with thee: thou hast holden me by my right hand. Thou shalt guide me with thy counsel, and afterward receive me to glory. Whom have I in heaven but thee? and there is none upon earth that I desire beside thee. My flesh and my heart faileth: but God is the strength of my heart, and my portion for ever. For, lo, they that are far from thee shall perish: thou hast destroyed all them that go a whoring from thee. But it is good for me to draw near to God. I have put my trust in the Lord God, that I may declare all thy works" (Psalm 73:2-28 in part).

Amos 3:3 asks, "Can two walk together, except they be *agreed?*" Therefore let man remember that if he *walks* with the wicked, he must *weep* with the wicked in hell. If he joins the wicked in sowing, he will also join in the reaping. We may see the wicked flourish and grow as the green grass and as the bay tree—but as the grass is soon cut down and as the green herb withers, so shall the wicked be! They may draw the sword against the righteous and mock and sneer at God's people; but at the appointed time God will judge the wicked in righteousness. They may become fat for awhile, but they will be utterly cut off when God sends judgment upon them, and the smoke of their torment will ascend up forever and ever:

"And I beheld when he had opened the sixth seal, and, lo, there was a great earthquake; and the sun became black as sackcloth of hair, and the moon became as blood; and the stars of heaven fell unto the earth, even as a fig tree casteth her untimely figs, when she is shaken of a mighty wind. And the heaven departed as a scroll when it is rolled together; and every mountain and island were moved out of their places. And the kings of the earth, and the great men, and the rich men, and the chief captains, and the mighty men, and every bondman, and every free man, hid themselves in the dens and in the rocks of the mountains; and said to the mountains and rocks, *Fall on us, and HIDE US from the face of Him that sitteth on the throne, and from THE WRATH OF THE LAMB:* for the great day of His wrath is come; and who shall be able to stand?" (Rev. 6:12-17).

"And the third angel followed them, saying with a loud voice, If any man worship the beast and his image, and receive his mark in his forehead, or in his hand, the same shall drink of the wine of the wrath of God, which is poured out without mixture into the cup of His indignation; and he shall be tormented with fire and brimstone in the presence of the holy angels, and in the presence of the Lamb: and the smoke of their torment ascendeth up for ever and ever: and they have no rest day nor night, who worship the beast and his image, and whosoever receiveth the mark of his name" (Rev. 14:9-11).

The clearest, most understandable sermon ever preached on hell was preached by the One who died that "whosoever will" might be saved and miss hell's damnation. In Mark 9:43-48 Jesus declared:

"If thy hand offend thee, cut it off: it is better for thee to enter into life maimed, than having two hands to go into hell, into the fire that never shall be quenched: where their worm dieth not, and the fire is not quenched. And if thy foot offend thee, cut it off: it is better for thee to enter halt into life, than having two feet to be cast into hell, into the fire that never shall be quenched: where their worm dieth not, and the fire is not quenched. And if thine eye offend thee, pluck it out: it is better for thee to enter into the kingdom of God with one eye, than having two eyes to be cast into hell fire: where their worm dieth not, and the fire is not quenched!"

This message from the lips of the Son of God needs no comment, it is self-explanatory: *hell is a horrible place!*

The End of the Righteous

"The meek shall inherit the earth; and shall delight themselves in the abundance of peace. . . . They shall not be ashamed in the evil time: and in the days of famine they shall be satisfied. . . . The Lord loveth judgment and forsaketh not His saints; they are preserved for ever. . . . Mark the perfect man, and behold the upright: for the end of that man is peace. . . . The salvation of the righteous is of the Lord: He is their strength in the time of trouble. And the Lord shall help them, and deliver them: He shall deliver them from the wicked, and save them, because they trust in Him."

These facts concerning the righteous are declared in the Psalm we have used for our text in this message. What a contrast to the statements made in the same Psalm concerning the wicked and their final doom!

Peter said to Jesus, "Behold, we have forsaken all, and followed thee. What shall we have therefore?" Jesus replied, "Verily I say unto you, That ye which have followed me, in the regeneration when the Son of man shall sit in the throne of His glory, ye also shall sit upon twelve thrones, judging the twelve tribes of Israel. And every one that hath forsaken houses, or brethren, or sisters, or father, or mother, or wife, or children, or lands, for my name's sake, shall receive *an hundredfold,* and shall inherit everlasting life" (Matt. 19:27-29). It is indeed true, as the Psalmist declared, that *"a little* that a *righteous* man hath is better than *the riches of many wicked!"* (Psalm 37:16).

The believer may have only the bare necessities

of life, he may never prosper in the things of this world. But when we consider the brevity of life on earth and the unending span of eternity, why should we fret or worry because the unrighteous may be more prosperous and have more good things in this life than we have?

James compares the brevity of life to a vapour, "that appeareth for a little time, and then vanisheth away" (James 4:14).

Peter tells us, "All flesh is as grass, and all the glory of man as the flower of grass. The grass withereth, and the flower thereof falleth away: but the Word of the Lord endureth for ever" (I Pet. 1:24, 25).

The Psalmist declares, "As for man, his days are as grass: as a flower of the field, so he flourisheth. For the wind passeth over it, and it is gone; and the place thereof shall know it no more. But the mercy of the Lord is from everlasting to everlasting upon them that fear Him . . ." (Psalm 103:15-17).

So what if we suffer awhile in this world? Paul declares that "the sufferings of this present time are not worthy to be compared with the GLORY which shall be revealed in us!" (Rom. 8:18). "Weeping may endure for a night, but JOY cometh in the morning" (Psalm 30:5). He who promised, "I will come again, and receive you unto myself" (John 14:3) will *keep* His promise; and when we see His face we will remember former things no more, regardless of how much we have suffered in this life, or how little of this world's goods may have been ours. "The Lord upholdeth the righteous . . . the Lord upholdeth him with His hand" (Psalm 37:17, 24). The righteous will never be forsaken or condemned, and the end of the righteous is peace.

Fellow Christian, I beseech you, *"Fret not!"* Declare with Job, "Though He *slay* me, yet will I trust in Him" (Job 13:15). If things are not as you would like them to be, if prayer has not been answered in exactly the way you expected, if trials and tribulations are pressing in upon you, remember that God is able and He knows the end in the beginning. Do not bow to doubt, discouragement, and fear—that is exactly what the devil wants you to do!

Shadrach, Meshach, and Abednego, facing the fiery furnace, said to Nebuchadnezzar, *"Our God . . . is able to deliver us* from the burning fiery furnace, and He will deliver us out of thine hand, O king. *BUT IF NOT, be it known unto thee, O king, that we WILL NOT serve thy gods, nor worship the golden image which thou hast set up."* The three Hebrews were cast into the furnace—but when the king looked again he saw *four* men walking in the fire, *and the form of the fourth was "like the SON OF GOD."* When the three men who had been thrown into the furnace were brought forth, the fire had had no power on their bodies, not a hair of their head was singed, their garments were not burned, and not even the smell of fire clung to them! (Read Daniel chapter 3.)

Our God is able today to deliver us from any trial, any "fiery furnace" we may be facing. BUT IF NOT—if it be not His will to deliver us—then He will go with us every step of the way through whatever He permits to come our way; and it has been my experience that for every trial He brings us through, we come forth with stronger faith, more humility—more *mature Christians*. Peter explains it this way:

"Wherein ye greatly rejoice, though now for a season, if need be, ye are in heaviness through manifold temptations: that the trial of your faith, being much more precious than of gold that perisheth, though it be tried with fire, might be found unto praise and honour and glory at the appearing of Jesus Christ" (I Pet. 1:6, 7).

For example, *Joseph* would never have reached a place of power in the land of Egypt if his brethren had not sold him into Egyptian slavery (Gen. 37:24-28; 41:41-44). What seemed certain disaster became tremendous blessing—not only to Joseph, but to his brethren as well.

Samson would not have had his hunger satisfied with the honey from the carcass of the lion had he not first met and overcome the lion (Judges 14:5-9).

Esther would not have been such a blessing to her people had it not been for the wicked Haman and his plotting against the queen and God's chosen nation (Esther 9:24, 25).

The *Apostle Paul* had a "thorn in the flesh." He testified, "For this thing I besought the Lord thrice, that it might depart from me. And He said unto me, *MY GRACE is sufficient for thee:* for my strength is made perfect in weakness. Most gladly therefore will I rather glory in my infirmities, that the power of Christ may rest upon me. Therefore I take pleasure in infirmities, in reproaches, in necessities, in persecutions, in distresses for Christ's sake: for when I am weak, then am I strong" (II Cor. 12:7-10).

Jesus despised the shame of the cross; but He endured its horror and suffering for the joy that was set before Him. The cross of Christ opened the door to His returning to the right hand of the Father, and eventually to His throne (Heb. 12:2; Luke 24:26).

We cannot see what lies ahead as God can see. Therefore the part of the righteous is simply to trust and obey. *God's* part is to supply our every need. How wonderful and blessed it is to realize our own nothingness and God's all-sufficiency! All things are ours in Jesus, for God the Father has given all things into His hands (John 3:35). We are not to trust Jesus for salvation from sin only, but for all else besides—strength, guidance, deliverance—every need is met in Him. We are "as having nothing, and yet *possessing ALL THINGS*" (II Cor. 6:10). We surrender to Jesus our nothingness—and in return we receive His all-sufficiency. In the words of the grand old hymn, "Nothing in my hand I bring, simply to thy cross I cling!"

But we are not to enjoy all of these blessings simply for ourselves. "God is able to make all grace abound toward you; *that ye, always having all sufficiency in all things, may abound to EVERY GOOD WORK*" (II Cor. 9:8). In other words, *all things are mine EXCEPT MYSELF!* I am not my own, I am bought with a price. Therefore it is my duty to glorify God—in my body, in my spirit, in all that I am and in all that I do. I belong to God (I Cor. 6:19, 20; Rom. 12:1).

"The meek shall inherit the earth; and shall delight themselves in the abundance of peace" (Psalm 37:11). The Psalmist here speaks of the millennial reign of Christ here on earth, when the saints will reign with Him. At that time, the wicked will have been overthrown, the knowledge of the Lord will cover the earth as the waters cover the sea, and in those glorious days there will be an *"abundance of peace."* The redeemed will then enjoy the pleasures God intended righteous men to enjoy.

"The earth is the Lord's, and the fulness thereof; the world, and they that dwell therein" (Psalm 24:1), but Satan and sin have caused tears, heartache, death, destruction, and misery. The earth will be delivered from the curse of sin during the glorious thousand-year reign of Christ, and the righteous will reign with Him. Truly, *"the sufferings of this present time are not worthy to be compared with the glory which shall be revealed in us!"*

The Sevenfold Commission
Given to the Righteous

In Psalm 37, quoted in our text, we find the sevenfold commission to the righteous, given by the Holy Spirit and penned down by David:

1. "Trust in the Lord, and do good; so shalt thou dwell in the land, and verily thou shalt be fed" (v. 3).

"Fret not"—but trust in the Lord. Believe His Word. Believing is faith, and faith is the victory that overcomes the world (I John 5:4). God cannot lie, His Word cannot be broken (Heb. 6:18; Tit. 1:2). We rest in Him who conquered the world, the flesh, the devil, death, hell, and the grave, and who now lives at the right hand of God to make intercession for us. He has never asked one of His children to face anything He did not face before us. He conquered all, and we are more than conquerors through Him. "If God be for us, who can be against us?" (Rom. 8:31). Therefore—"trust in the Lord . . . do good"—and leave the rest to Him, resting on His promise "so shalt thou dwell in the land, and verily thou shalt be fed!"

2. "Delight thyself also in the Lord—and He shall give thee the desires of thine heart" (v. 4).

This goes beyond merely *trusting*. To *delight* in

145

the Lord means to make Him our treasure, our joy, our life. We may never acquire many material things, though we may see the wicked prosper around us. But in the Lord we possess *all things.* Therefore we are to *delight in Him.* In Romans 5:1-10 Paul points out the seven glorious results of being justified by faith, and then in verse 11 he adds, "and not only so, but *we also JOY IN GOD through our Lord Jesus Christ,* by whom we have now received the atonement."

Whatever the believer may have or may not have, *he has CHRIST;* and in Him all things are added (Matt. 6:33; Col. 2:10). God has called us into the fellowship of His dear Son, Christ Jesus. Let us make Him our joy and our delight, praising Him for all things, knowing that in God's eternal plan all things work together for good to those who love God and are called according to His purpose.

3. *"Commit thy way unto the Lord;* trust also in Him; and He shall bring it to pass" (v. 5).

To commit something into the care of another means to *surrender* or *consign* that "something" for safekeeping, and implies that whatever is given over passes entirely into another's charge. This is what Paul meant when in his second letter to young Timothy he testified, *"I know WHOM I have believed,* and am persuaded that He is *able to keep that which I have COMMITTED UNTO HIM against that day"* (II Tim. 1:12).

So completely did Paul commit his all to Christ

that he could declare, ". . . I have learned, in *whatsoever* state I am, therewith to be *content*. I know both how to be abased, and I know how to abound: everywhere and in all things I am instructed both to be full and to be hungry, both to abound and to suffer need. *I can do ALL THINGS through Christ which strengtheneth me*" (Phil. 4:11-13). What could bring more peace, more freedom from anxiety, than to *commit our WAY* unto the Lord, trusting Him to direct our steps and bring to pass whatever is for our good and His glory?

4. "*Rest* in the Lord . . ." (v. 7).

The Hebrew word here translated "rest" means "be *silent* in the Lord," be *still* before God. Rest, in faith believing, and God will bring to pass all that He has promised. Cease from looking at man, trusting in man, or fretting about man. Cease from self. Jesus took our place and endured all that sin and hell could heap upon anyone. Believers are IN Christ (Col. 3:3), therefore we need only *rest* in Him and know that whatever He does for us is what is best.

5. ". . . *wait patiently* for Him" (v. 7).

That is, *stand* upon Him. Let Him be your foundation, the chief cornerstone of your life, the Rock of Ages. "The Stone which the builders rejected, the same is become the head of the corner" (Matt. 21:42). Christ is that Stone, and in I Corinthians 3:11 Paul tells us, "Other foundation can no

147

man lay than that is laid, which is Jesus Christ."
It is upon Christ the Solid Rock that we are to
stand, with patience, and await His will and do
His bidding. We are not to ask, "Where is the
promise of His coming?" because He who declared,
"I will come" *will come* at the appointed hour.
Therefore we need be anxious for nothing, "but in
every thing by prayer and supplication *with thanks-
giving* let your requests be made known unto God.
And the peace of God, which passeth all under-
standing, shall keep your hearts and minds through
Christ Jesus" (Phil. 4:6, 7).

6. *". . . wait upon the Lord . . ."* (v. 9).

"Wait" here is used in the same sense that the
Thessalonians "turned to God from idols to serve
the living and true God, and *to WAIT FOR HIS
SON from heaven . . ."* (I Thess. 1:9, 10). Thus
"waiting" carries the thought of *hope*. This is
what every believer must do. As children of God
we must wait for the time of our deliverance, because God works according to the appointed time
in His eternal plan and program. So we *wait,*
"looking for *that blessed HOPE,* and the glorious
appearing of the great God and our Saviour Jesus
Christ" (Tit. 2:13).

7. *"Wait on the Lord, and keep His way,* and
He shall exalt thee to inherit the land . . ."* (v. 34).

This speaks of that glorious day when Jesus will
come to reward His servants according to their
faithful stewardship. Thus are the righteous com-

missioned to *trust* in the Lord, *delight* in the Lord, *commit our way* unto the Lord, *rest* in the Lord, *wait patiently* on the Lord, *wait upon the Lord* that we may *inherit the earth,* wait on the Lord and *keep His way* that He may exalt us in due time.

This tells us that we are not to run ahead of God or make our own plans and then ask His approval. We are not to fret or become discouraged when we think God has not acted as quickly as we hoped or expected. God expects us to trust Him completely, rest in Him and stand on His Word. *"Forever, O Lord, thy Word is settled in heaven"* (Psalm 119:89).

Dear reader, can you say with Paul, *"I KNOW whom I have believed?"* Do you know beyond any doubt that you are truly born again and that God numbers you among His "righteous"? If you know you are a child of God, then trust in Him with all your heart and be not anxious, knowing that He doeth all things well. Such faith can be had only by *reading and appropriating* the Word of God. If you are a believer but you do not have victory in your Christian life, study the Word. Feed upon it. Trust completely in the Lord, commit your way unto Him, and wait patiently for Him to fulfill that which He has promised.

If you are *not* sure of your salvation, or if you know you are not saved, then God grant that you put off salvation no longer! *"NOW is the accepted time . . . NOW is the day of salvation"* (II Cor. 6:2). God warns, "Boast not thyself of to morrow; for thou knowest not what a day may bring forth" (Prov. 27:1). You have this moment, today. Before this day ends you may go out into eternity to stand before God. You cannot afford to meet Him without Christ!

Will you read the following verses, do what they tell you to do, and then bow your head and ask God to save you for Jesus' sake?

John 1:12, 13: "As many as received Him, to them gave He power to become the sons of God, even to them that believe on His name: which were born—not of blood, nor of the will of the flesh, nor of the will of man—*but of GOD.*"

John 3:18, 36: "He that believeth on Him is not condemned: but he that believeth not is condemned already, because he hath not believed in the name of the only begotten Son of God. . . . He that believeth on the Son hath everlasting life: and he that believeth not the Son shall not see life; but the wrath of God abideth on him."

John 5:24: "Verily, verily, I say unto you, He that heareth my Word, and believeth on Him that sent me, hath everlasting life, and shall not come into condemnation; but is passed from death unto life."

Acts 16:31: "Believe on the Lord Jesus Christ, and thou shalt be saved, and thy house."

Romans 10:9, 10: "If thou shalt confess with thy

mouth the Lord Jesus, and shalt believe in thine heart that God hath raised Him from the dead, thou shalt be saved. For with the heart man believeth unto righteousness; and with the mouth confession is made unto salvation."

I John 5:10-15: "He that believeth on the Son of God hath the witness in himself: he that believeth not God hath made Him a liar; because he believeth not the record that God gave of His Son. And this is the record, that God hath given to us eternal life, and this life is in His Son. He that hath the Son hath life; and he that hath not the Son of God hath not life.

"These things have I written unto you that believe on the name of the Son of God; *that ye may KNOW that ye have eternal life,* and that ye may believe on the name of the Son of God. And this is the confidence that we have in Him, that, if we ask any thing according to His will, He heareth us: and if we know that He hear us, whatsoever we ask, we know that we have the petitions that we desired of Him."

I urge you to take God at His Word. Invite Jesus to come into your heart. *Believe*—and because God has spoken, the miracle will occur in your heart and the Holy Spirit will bear witness that you are a child of God.

My prayer is that this message will bless all who read it, and that many souls may be led to accept Jesus and be born again!